ERRATUM

TROTSKY David King

The illustrations on pages 235 and 281
have been transposed.

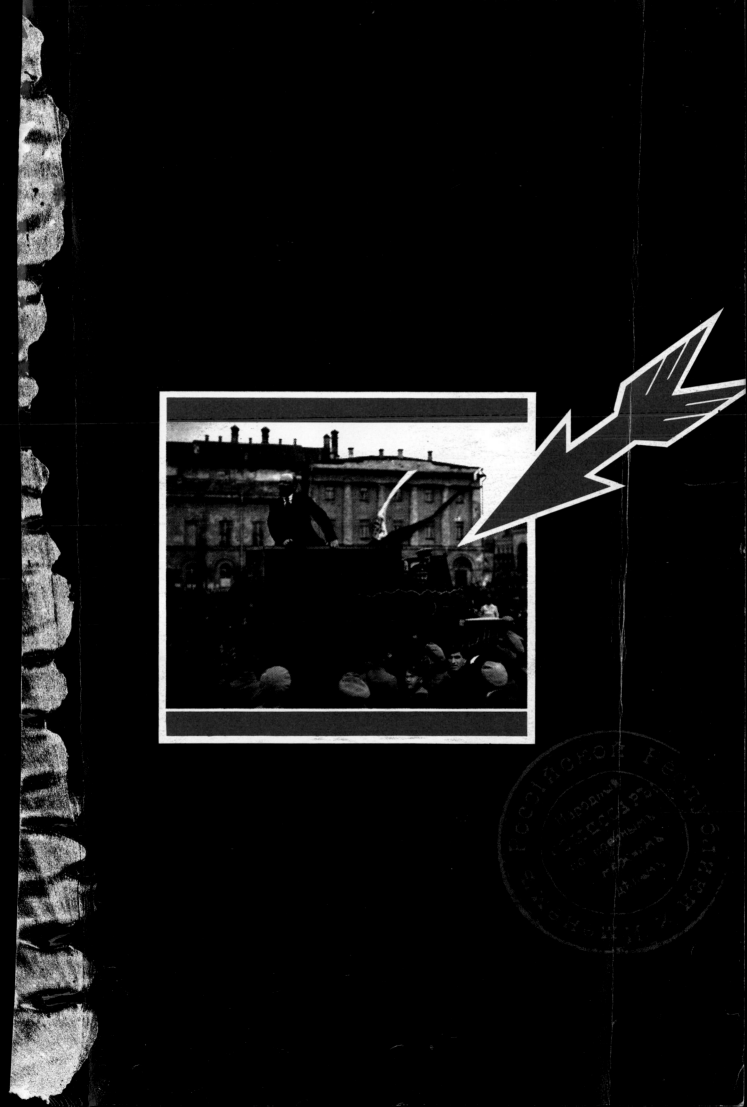

TROTSKY

A PHOTOGRAPHIC BIOGRAPHY BY DAVID KING

COMMENTARY BY JAMES RYAN

INTRODUCTION BY TAMARA DEUTSCHER

BASIL BLACKWELL
OXFORD AND NEW YORK

DESIGNED BY DAVID KING

TROTSKY

First published 1986
Copyright   David King 1986
Introduction   Tamara Deutscher 1986
Commentary   James Ryan 1986

Basil Blackwell Ltd
108 Cowley Road, Oxford OX4 1JF, UK

Basil Blackwell Inc.
432 Park Avenue South, Suite 1505,
New York, NY 10016, USA

British Library Cataloguing in Publication Data
Trotsky: a photographic biography.
1. Trot'ski-ĭ, L.
2. Revolutionists — Soviet Union — Biography
3. Statesmen — Soviet Union — Biography
I. King, David, 1943–
II. Ryan, James
947.084'1'0924   DK254.T6
ISBN 0 – 631 – 14689 – X

Library of Congress Cataloging in Publication Data
King, David, 1943–
Trotsky: a photographic biography.
1. Trotsky, Leon, 1879 – 1940 — Portraits, caricatures, etc.
I. Title.
DK254.T6K56 1986 947.084'092'4   85 – 13462
ISBN 0 – 631 – 14689 – X

Printed in Hong Kong

PHOTOGRAPHS FROM THE DAVID KING COLLECTION

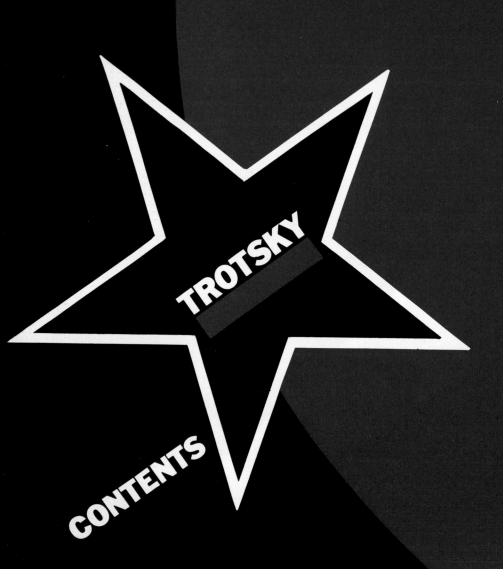

CONTENTS

TROTSKY

FOR GEORGE L.WEISSMAN

(1916-1985)

PREFACE

On 7 March 1935 a directive was issued by the Central Committee of the Communist Party ordering the removal of all Trotsky's works from libraries throughout the Soviet Union. Being caught in possession of any material, written or photographic, on or by Trotsky or 'Trotskyites' was an offence during the years of the Great Terror punishable by banishment to the hideous twilight world of Stalin's Gulag empire, where final destruction was almost certainly assured. The systematic extermination of literally millions of people denounced as Trotskyists or 'enemies of the people' was the culmination of Stalin's campaign against revolutionary communism which began during the power struggle following Lenin's death.

Today there is still no trace of Trotsky in the Soviet Union. His name is not mentioned, his photographs are banned, his writings are suppressed, he has been eradicated from the history books, and, of course, a volume such as this would be seized immediately as anti-Soviet propaganda. The same is true of all the nations which profess to being 'Communist'. More than four decades after his assassination his works are still illegal literature across half the globe. The ideas of world revolution, which the co-leader of the October insurrection and founder of the Red Army put forth, are concepts that today's rulers in Moscow, and their imitators elsewhere, cannot bear to contemplate, following as they do in Stalin's footsteps, shackled to the chauvinistic doctrine of 'socialism in one country'.

In the West, matters are only a little better. Since Trotsky dedicated his life to the overthrow of capitalism, it is not surprising that most people in capitalist countries know his name only as a term of abuse through disinformation in the media.

This book is the culmination of sixteen years of researching rare photographs, many from friends and associates of Trotsky, scattered throughout Europe, America and Mexico. The accompanying text, which follows Tamara Deutscher's distinguished introduction, has been carefully structured by James Ryan to parallel the photographs throughout, so that the book might be read in the same way as seeing a documentary film. Here is the visual proof of the extraordinary life of the world's most brilliant 'permanent revolutionary'.

David King

ACKNOWLEDGEMENTS

Most of the visual material reproduced in this book comes from the David King Collection of photographs, posters, photographic albums, books and journals on twentieth-century Russia. The material on Trotsky has been collected mainly from his friends and associates in Europe and America. Special thanks are due to Francis Wyndham, the late George L. Weissman, Tamara Deutscher, Judy Groves, Professor Stephen F. Cohen, Louis Sinclair and René Olivieri for their support, inspiration and tireless encouragement. Gratitude is also expressed to the following for their kind assistance in the task of tracing the photographs: Estaban Volkov; the late Herman Axelbank; Marguerite Bonnet; George Breitman; Pierre Broué; the late Walter Goldwater; Ronald Gray; David Weston, curator of the Trotsky collection at Glasgow University Library; Anthony C. Hall; Jean van Heijenoort; the late Sara Jacobs; the late Michael Katanka; Richard Davies of the Leeds Russian Archive; the Brotherton Collection at the University of Leeds; Bert Patenaude; the late Max Shachtman; Magnum Photos; and SPADEM. Special thanks are due to Colin Smith, Nick Robin, Sue Macdonald, Hilary Driver and Kathy Shawcross for excellent technical photographic assistance and typesetting, and to Sarah Bourne for reading the text in draft and proof. The remarkable effort and unstinting enthusiasm of James Ryan in writing the text and captions cannot be overvalued. **D.K.**

It was the historian Isaac Deutscher who made it possible for the facts of Trotsky's life to be told. His unrivalled three-volume biography, published by Oxford University Press between 1954 and 1963, has been our starting point and constant guide. We have also been able to draw on the published recollections of many of Trotsky's comrades and fellow revolutionaries; among them have been those of his wife Natalya Sedova, Victor Serge, Alfred Rosmer, Nadezhda Krupskaya, Fyodor Raskolnikov, A.F. Ilyin-Zhenevsky, Erich Wollenberg, John Reed, Louise Bryant, Ante Ciliga, Jean van Heijenoort, Julian Gorkin, Joseph Hansen, and the anonymous authors of Vorkhuta, and others are cited in the text. In 1925 Max Eastman wrote a portrait of the young revolutionary (to 1903), and Trotsky himself published an autobiography covering his life to 1929. The historical writings of Marcel Liebman, Moshe Lewin and E.H. Carr have also provided valuable insights into episodes in Trotsky's life.

There have been two immediate antecedents to the present work. In 1972 Penguin published 'Trotsky: A Documentary' by Francis Wyndham and David King, and in 1979 a French edition with expanded photographic content by David King and text by Pierre Broué was published by EDI in Paris. A tremendous debt is owed especially to Francis Wyndham's pioneering research.

Almost all of these works are, or have recently been, available in English. Even more importantly, since it is through direct contact with his ideas that his political significance can be appreciated, translations of a large proportion of Trotsky's own writings can be found. Credit for this goes in the first place to Pathfinder Press, who have collected many of his shorter writings between 1929 and 1940 into fourteen volumes and have separately produced most of his major works. Others have been published under the Monad imprint, or by New Park, Pluto and Penguin.

Above all, the continuing relevance of unfalsified revolutionary Marxism — Trotskyism — has inspired the writing in this book. It is to be hoped that our account of Trotsky's contributions to the preservation and development of communism as the hope for the future of humanity will help to perpetuate that tradition. **J.R.**

War Commissar Leon Trotsky with one of his aides,
I. Impazmin (right), and Central
Committee member Alexei Rykov (centre)
at a demonstration in honour of the
Second Congress of the Communist International,
Moscow, spring 1920.

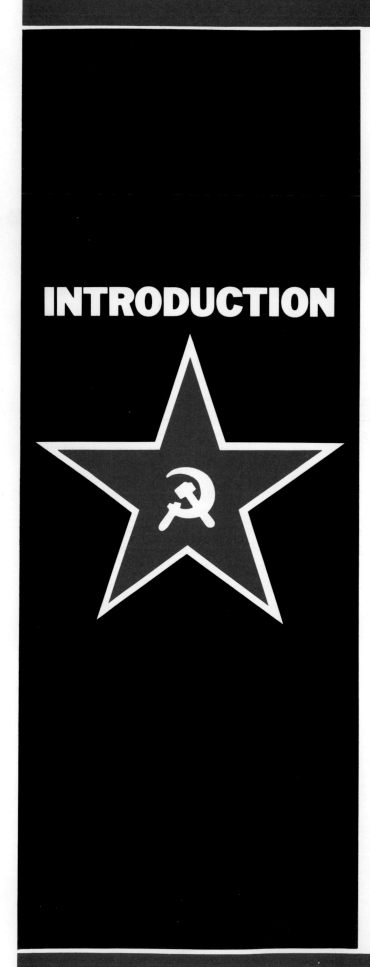

INTRODUCTION

'When I first began to draft these memoirs, it often seemed to me as if I were not writing of my own childhood but of a long-past journey into a distant land' — thus Trotsky in the opening chapter of his autobiography. And indeed, the world of his adult life was divided from that of his early years 'not only in time and space by decades and by far countries, but by the mountain chain of great events'.

He was born on 26 October 1879 in the province of Kherson in the sunlit and wide-open spaces of the fertile Southern Ukrainian steppe. Thirty-eight years later to the very day, on 26 October (7 November according to the new calendar) 1917, he was to lead the Bolshevik insurrection in Petrograd, the insurrection which proved to be the highest peak in the 'mountain chain of great events' of the twentieth century. He was laid to rest far away from his native steppe, far away from the scene of his revolutionary triumphs of the great October days. A white stone marks his simple grave in a shady garden of a suburban villa in Mexico City. He died at the age of 60, killed by an assassin sent to drive an ice-pick into his skull. The blood of the victim stained the pages of his manuscript narrating the life of the man who, immured in the Kremlin, masterminded the murder.

Trotsky's deadly antagonist was born in the same year, though in quite different circumstances. On 21 December 1879 in Gori, Georgia, in a dim one-room dwelling Ekaterina Djugashvili gave birth to a boy named Joseph. His father, Vissarion, was a cobbler. His propensity to drink did not improve the fortunes of the family and may have contributed to his early death when his son was barely 11. His wife, Ekaterina, the daughter of a serf, had already at the age of 20 given birth to three children, but they all died in infancy. Joseph, affectionately called Soso, seemed to be healthy, lively and strong. Under the name of Joseph Stalin he was to enter history as the absolute and grim ruler of the far-flung Soviet Union, weighing on the fate of millions all over the world.

The momentous feud, reminiscent of Greek tragedies, between the Georgian cobbler's son — the master of all the Russias — and Trotsky, the hero of the greatest revolution of our century, lasted for decades. The future may transcend the bloody conflict between the victorious Stalin and the defeated Trotsky, but the principles, theories and hopes which Trotsky advanced, to which he gave such an artistic and consummate form, have for ever enriched the history of ideas.

Lev Davidovich Bronstein was the youngest child of a well-to-do Jewish farmer. It was unusual for Jews to take up farming, and not many managed to leave the ghetto to which they had been confined by the Tsarist laws; only those who had in them some pioneering spirit were attracted by the wilderness near the Black Sea. The family was hard-working and thrifty. Unlike many farmers, but like many Jews, they had enormous respect for learning and were ambitious for their children: they were determined to give them a university education. By the time the youngest boy, named after the grandfather Lev or Lyova, was born, the farm was prospering and the children's future seemed to be secure.

Like Marx, Engels and Lenin, Trotsky was not drawn to socialism by the conditions of his own existence. He might have witnessed cruel social injustice on his father's farm; he could not have failed to notice it in his adolescence in Odessa, the Russian Marseilles, the southern port of rich merchants, where the poor were very poor and there were many of them. He belonged to the privileged and recoiled from the sight of misery. It was not the study of society that at first aroused his interest, but of mathematics which seemed to him to possess 'not only truth but supreme beauty'. He enrolled at the University of Odessa. But in the Russia of Nicholas II all seats of learning were hotbeds of revolutionary agitation, and the young Bronstein was soon caught up in political ferment and activity. At first he defended the cause of the Narodniks (Populists) whose heroic and romantic tradition appealed to him — but not for long. 'How on earth can a young girl, so full of life, stand that dry, narrow, impractical stuff,' he exclaimed. The 'dry, narrow, impractical stuff' was the Marxist doctrine which was gaining ground among the rebellious youth; the 'young girl so full of life' was Alexandra Sokolovskaya, whom he was soon to marry.

The initial spell of Bronstein's clandestine activity lasted only a few months. He got his first taste of Tsarist prison in 1897. By 1899, at the age of 20, he already had a year and a half of solitary confinement behind him, and a year later, together with myriads of other revolutionaries, he was deported to Siberia. His wife went with him. In her arms she carried a baby daughter, Zina, wrapped in thick furs to protect her from the cold. They travelled on sledges in the middle of a severe winter with temperatures of 90 degrees below freezing point.

Alexandra had no doubt that her husband was destined for greatness and that at 23 it was time for him to do something for mankind. She was prepared to brave the rigours of the banishment on her own, with the two-year-old Zina and the newly born Nina. She urged him to escape. For the benefit of the policeman who checked daily on the deportees, a dummy was left in his bed. He managed to reach Irkutsk, where an underground organization provided him with a false passport; hastily he scribbled on it the name of his former jailer — Trotsky — a name destined to loom so large in the annals of history.

His four and a half years in prison and exile were by no means wasted. His mind and his pen were more active than ever before. Enamoured of European literature, he wrote innumerable essays on Nietzsche, Zola, Ruskin and Maupassant as well as on Herzen, Belinsky and other great and influential Russian thinkers. He was a literary critic by vocation. And literary criticism, which afforded a refuge from the assaults of censorship, was for him a vehicle to convey his political views. On his trek from Siberia to the West he found that his literary reputation had preceded him. In one of the clandestine centres a message from Lenin awaited him: the young Bronstein, nicknamed 'The Pen', was to join him in London.

And indeed one morning, almost at dawn, in October 1902 he appeared at the doorstep of Lenin and his wife Krupskaya who, as Mr and Mrs Richter, lived in Holford Square, near Kings Cross. Straightway he was put to work on the journal 'Iskra' ('The Spark') together with such pioneers of socialism as Plekhanov and Vera Zasulich. Zasulich was a legendary figure: a year before Trotsky's birth she had fired at the Tsarist General Trepov. After the jury had acquitted her, she fled abroad. She kept in touch with Marx and, though not fully accepting his teaching, she was regarded as one of the founders of the Russian Marxist school.

In 'Iskra' the 'young eagle' wrote in a somewhat flamboyant and romantic style, which Lenin with tact and patience tried to prune. Soon, however, not matters of style but deep political disagreements shattered the solidarity of the 'Iskra' team. In July 1903 at the stormy Second Congress of the Russian Social Democratic Party, in a drab warehouse at the back of the Maison du Peuple in Brussels, the historic split into Bolsheviks and Mensheviks occurred. Ostensibly the break came over paragraph 1 of the party statutes. Lenin demanded that the party be a closely knit and highly disciplined body of active revolutionaries, while Martov, another prominent 'Iskra' editor, envisaged a looser association of men and women who merely assisted the underground organization without necessarily being bound by any organizational ties. After protracted and acrimonious debates Lenin won the day by a majority of two votes. His followers were labelled Bolsheviks (the men of the majority) while those of Martov became known as the Mensheviks (the minority). It was an irony of history that Plekhanov, who later became an irreconcilable enemy of Bolshevism and the revolution, then sided with Lenin, while Trotsky, who died an unrepentant Bolshevik, was Lenin's most strident opponent.

Already in 1901, in exile, before he ever met Lenin, Trotsky had argued on the same 'Leninist' lines. Yet, when faced with the actual choice, he opted for the Mensheviks. He did not stay with them long, but long enough to express his hostility to Lenin, which was as violent as it was sudden. He assailed Lenin with all the flourish of his invective, hurling at him epithets full of personal venom. Isaac Deutscher, Trotsky's biographer, remarked that in this Trotsky 'exhibited a characteristic of which he would never quite free himself: he could not separate ideas from men'.

Immediately after the congress, with the heat of the battle still in his blood, he wrote his 'anti-Bolshevik' indictment of Lenin, a document which he was grievously to regret all his life. But among the welter of contradictory and odd statements we find in it this clear-sighted and uncanny prophecy: 'The party organization would at first ... substitute itself for the party as a whole; then the Central Committee would substitute itself for the organization; and finally a single "dictator" would substitute himself for the Central Committee ... '

After a short Menshevik phase Trotsky remained for a time organizationally unattached. He was repelled by the Mensheviks' nerveless middle-class liberalism, but there was too much visionary romanticism in him to allow him to embrace the spare discipline demanded by Lenin. He was now at odds with most of the émigré groups, and although as a speaker and lecturer he was in great demand and although a substantial flow of articles, essays and pamphlets was coming from his pen, he became as fretful in his comfortable West European exile as he had been in the wilderness of Siberia only a few short years before. He watched intensely from afar the political scene in Russia, where he detected a new groundswell of revolutionary ferment.

In January 1905 the workers of Petersburg, with their wives and children, led by Father Gapon, a prison chaplain, marched in an enormous procession to the Winter Palace. Chanting and carrying aloft the Tsar's portraits, holy icons and church banners, they wanted to submit to the Tsar a petition begging that he should help them in their misery and redress their grievances. The gates of the palace remained closed. The crowd was met with bullets. There were many dead and wounded. The guards' fire ignited a revolutionary explosion. 'The proletarians of Petersburg have shown great heroism. But the unarmed heroism of the crowd could not face the armed ideology of the barracks,' commented Trotsky. The temper of the working class was hot and impulsive. Russia was about to erupt and Trotsky was irresistibly attracted to the centre of the storm.

He returned to Petersburg in February and immediately plunged — under all sorts of assumed names — into clandestine activity while most of the other socialist leaders were still in Western Europe. He no longer lectured small groups of émigrés, but harangued thousands and thousands of workers filling the streets and squares of Kiev, Minsk and Petersburg. Though the turmoil of January and February was over, the rumblings of the next wave of unrest were clearly heard. The Soviet or Council of Workers' Deputies made its appearance, and, as the first popular elective body, gained immediately an extraordinary authority.

The hub of the expanding revolution was the Petersburg Soviet and as President of its Executive Leon Trotsky set the wheels in motion. But the time was not ripe. The workers were not organized and were inexperienced. On 3 December 1905 the fifty glorious days of the Petersburg Soviet came to an end. An officer at the head of a detachment of soldiers entered the hall and read the warrant of arrest. He was stopped midsentence by the exuberant President of the Executive who declared that the business of the session was not yet over. However, recognizing the futility of armed resistance, the Soviet had finally to submit to the forces of 'law and order'. But Trotsky had the last word: 'The meeting of the Executive is closed,' he declared solemnly. After that the delegates were marched off to prison.

The old régime was too weak to rule yet strong enough to defend itself. The 1905 revolution had been foredoomed. Trotsky made his mark, but spent himself in brilliant fireworks of oratory which stirred the masses, appealed to their imagination, and thereby furthered the cause of the revolution to come. Twelve years later he again assumed the post of the President of the Petersburg Soviet, but backed by the solid power and disciplined organization of the Bolshevik Party (which he then joined) he used his immense talents to greater effect. 1905 ended in defeat but it turned out to be the dress rehearsal for the victory of 1917.

The popularity and the prestige of the first soviet in history was so great that even under lock and key its members were accorded every privilege; and its chief spokesman was treated as an important prisoner of state. While outside the strikes and demonstrations were still threatening the régime, behind the prison walls Trotsky and his companions were feverishly preparing their defence. Martov on behalf of the Mensheviks was planning to plead the case of the soviets with moderation; Trotsky was determined to adopt a most defiant attitude and to use the dock as a political platform to state the revolutionary objectives of the soviets. Within the confines of the prison his mind was as active as ever. 'I sit and work and am quite sure that nobody can arrest me — in Tsarist Russia this is rather an unusual feeling', he said. He again produced a number of pamphlets and essays easily smuggled out of prison. He also pondered the 'Lessons of 1905' and sketched a prophetic vision of the great upheaval to come. From this period also dates his chief work, 'Results and Prospects' (subtitled 'The moving forces of the revolution'), which as the fundamental statement of 'Trotskyism' was to be the object of fierce controversy.

The trial, when it finally took place, lasted several weeks. Trotsky and fourteen other members of the Executive were sentenced to deportation to Siberia for life, and at dawn on 5 January 1907, dressed in grey prison clothes, they started on their trek. But Trotsky never reached his destination. While the newspapers of Petersburg were still carrying reports about the journey of the convicts towards the Polar Circle, Trotsky, with the help of other deportees, local peasants and guides, was galloping in the opposite direction.

Nineteen hundred and seven was the year of the Tsar's revenge. Autocracy was fully re-established. The reign of terror began. Courts martial and the gallows dominated the political scene. The revolutionary movement was at its nadir. It seemed that only dreamers and visionaries could withstand the all-pervading disillusionment and confusion. Only the boldest spirits remained faithful to their ideals. Only the strongest did not give up the struggle. With no possibility of action in the country, a new stream of émigrés was moving to the safety of western Europe.

Trotsky, accompanied by Natalya Sedova, his second wife whom he had met in Paris during his first exile, and their baby son Lyova, made their way to Vienna. There he spent most of the next seven years — the least tumultuous of his life. At the outbreak of the war he moved to Switzerland and then to Paris, where he divided his time between legal journalism — he wrote for the liberal 'Kievan Thought' — and revolutionary work among the political émigrés.

The one great event of those years in which Trotsky played a central part was the 1915 Zimmerwald Conference. This was a gathering of representatives of eleven countries, belligerent and neutral, who came together to protest against the war and to assert their socialist solidarity. Although the conference achieved little at the time, it became the forerunner of the Third — the Communist — International.

From Zimmerwald Trotsky returned to Paris and continued to send his reports to the 'Kievan Thought'. Earlier, during the Balkan war, he had acted as a military commentator and from an amateur soon changed into an expert on military affairs. Influenced by Clausewitz's strategic theories, he developed his own conceptions. Unlike most men concerned with war, he had a shrewd eye for the economic, political and social contexts masked by the clash of arms; he had a better feel for the morale of the embattled peoples; and he was more preoccupied with the nightmare of individual suffering. All this lifted his writings high above the merely professional level. The future Commissar of War, the builder of the Red Army, the commander-in-chief who was to defeat the 'Anti-Soviet Crusade of Fourteen Nations', was acquiring the knowledge and experience which to this day remain valid.

In the course of 1916 the Tsarist Embassy exerted more and more pressure on Russia's French ally; and the French police redoubled their zeal in curbing the activities of the anti-Tsarist émigrés in Paris. Trotsky had to leave France. He found asylum in the United States, and with his wife and two sons arrived in New York on 13 January 1917.

In the colony of Russian émigrés he was greeted with enthusiasm as the author of the Zimmerwald Manifesto. In their circles he became a popular speaker, and for the first time joined a distinctly Bolshevik paper edited by Bukharin and Alexandra Kollontai. His stay in America lasted barely two months, during which he saw the country growing richer and richer, while Europe was changing into a graveyard. Would Europe ever recover? Or 'will the world economic and cultural centre of gravity shift to America?', he asked.

In March of the same year the news of bread riots in Petrograd excited the émigré colony. The formation of the Provisional Government of Prince Lvov was greeted as the first step on the road to revolution; Trotsky was now forecasting that 'No human force will stem the powerful avalanche . . . ' until 'all the reactionary litter that has over centuries piled up around the Tsar's throne' was swept away. Prince Lvov and his ministers were part of that litter. Now it was time to grasp firmly the 'iron broom of history' and return to Petrograd.

After a long sea voyage and a spell of internment in the British camp in Canada, Trotsky at last arrived at the Russian frontier. In Petrograd, the scene of his previous triumph and defeat, he was met by an enthusiastic crowd flying red banners, who carried him shoulder high. To them he immediately addressed a call for revolution.

Lenin had returned to Petrograd a month earlier. Their roads now met. Both had, during the long separation, somewhat revised their views — indeed some Bolsheviks reproached Lenin with having abandoned Bolshevism for Trotskyism. Lenin never once mentioned the old controversies. But much, much later, when Lenin was no more, Stalin began persistently to throw them back at Trotsky in order to discredit him. The generous tribute which Lenin had paid soon after October to the commander of the uprising' was blotted [out from] the records of history, as was Lenin's remark [that si]nce Trotsky has broken with the Mensheviks, there has been no better Bolshevik.'

The position of the two men was, on the eve of the insurrection, quite different. Lenin was a recognized leader of a great and disciplined party; Trotsky and his friends were 'a pleiad of brilliant generals without an army' — but not for long. An orator of genius, he made his impact through the spoken word. Once again he joined the Executive of the Petrograd Soviet and set out to prepare, organize and lead the actual insurrection. Within only two or three weeks of his arrival in Russia he gained enormous popularity as the most eloquent agitator of the Soviet Left.

The naval base of Kronstadt became his favourite stamping ground. He was the author of the Red Sailors' fiery Manifesto, and the men of Kronstadt followed and guarded him as their idol. Later the Kronstadt base proved to be of extraordinary — almost symbolic — importance in his political fortunes.

He also established his platform in the huge Cirque Moderne, where every night he addressed jubilant audiences, in the midst of which he could often distinguish two adoring pairs of eyes: those of his teenage daughters from his first marriage. Sukhanov, a contemporary witness, thus described the scene: '... there were endless queues and crowds, whom the enormous amphitheatre could not contain ... Trotsky, breaking away from his work at the revolutionary headquarters, ran from the Obukhovsky to the Trubochnyi, from the Putilovsky to the Baltiinsky (the largest industrial plants in Petrograd), from the Manege to the barracks; and it seemed that he spoke everywhere simultaneously ... He was the central figure of those days, and the chief hero of this remarkable chapter of history.'

Outside the capital the disintegrating army suffered ever fresh defeats. The German navy was active in the Gulf of Finland and about to attack Petrograd. The Provisional Government was paralysed by fear: it was afraid of the German threat; it was equally frightened by the hot temper of the Red capital; and it toyed with the idea of moving to the less turbulent Moscow. The counter-revolution seemed to be in league with the national foe. The revolution had to defend itself against the enemy without and the enemy within.

On 9 October the Executive of the Soviet established the Military Revolutionary Committee — the supreme organ of the insurrection. 'Our government', declared Trotsky in front of enthusiastic soldiers and sailors, 'may flee from Petrograd. But the revolutionary people will not leave the city — it will defend it to the end.' On Trotsky's orders 5,000 rifles were passed from the arsenals to the civilian Red Guards. It was obvious that now the Military Revolutionary Committee could issue orders that were obeyed; it could overrule the established military organization. Unlike the rebels of 1905, the revolutionaries of 1917 were arming themselves for the decisive confrontation.

Lenin and Trotsky spent the night of 25 October in the Smolny Institute. Tired beyond endurance, tense, full of hopes and forebodings, they tried to get some sleep on the floor of a dark and empty room adjoining the Hall of the Soviets. Next morning Trotsky proclaimed the victory of the Bolshevik Revolution. Lenin, as the head of the ruling party, formed his first Soviet Government, and — to use his own expression — 'proceeded to build a new social order'.

The Bolsheviks assumed a prodigious burden of commitments in a backward country, ravaged by war, famine, age-old poverty and squalor. They had promised peace, bread and land.

As Commissar of Foreign Affairs, Trotsky was dispatched to Brest Litovsk to sue the Imperial German and Austrian generals for peace. The negotiations dragged on interminably. The Soviet Government loudly proclaimed its peace aims. It appealed over the heads of governments directly to the belligerent peoples calling upon them to rise, to lay down their arms, and to stop the war waged not in their interest but in that of their oppressors and exploiters. Belief in the imminence of European revolution was widespread among the Bolsheviks; indeed, they viewed the Russian revolution only as a prelude to a general European upheaval. The unrest among the German population, the political ferment in the army and sporadic revolts in the German navy nourished these hopes. Would the war be brought to an end by new revolutionary régimes or should the young Soviet republic come to terms with hostile capitalist rulers?

The further the vision of a socialist revolution in Europe receded, the harsher were the terms on which Russia could buy some peace and thus save her own revolution. The Bolsheviks had no option: the Russian army was practically non-existent. The great mass of soldiers 'voted for peace with their feet' and ran away from the front. Most of them had their roots in rural Russia and were eager to take part in the general assault on the landlords' estates.

The ink on the most humiliating and punitive peace agreement was hardly dry when new dangers beset the young republic. All counter-revolutionary forces — the White Guards and the White armies — joined hands with the fourteen nations which answered President Wilson's call for a crusade against the new communist state. Surrounded by her enemies, cut off from her granaries, Russia was disarmed and starving. The bread ration in Petersburg and Moscow was reduced to about one ounce a day.

In the middle of March 1918 Trotsky was appointed Commissar of War and President of the Supreme War Council. He now faced a task of herculean proportions: to conjure an army out of an apparent void. He harnessed all his passion, all his energy and all his inventiveness to the task. In October 1917 the Red Guards of Petrograd and Moscow numbered 7,000 fully armed men; two and a half years later the Red Army had five million men under arms. The civil war was raging all around the shrinking territory on which the writ of the Soviets still ran. The army had to fight on

fronts with a circumference of over 5,000 miles. Trotsky conducted the operations from his military train, which became legendary. He travelled incessantly and seemed to be in all centres of crisis simultaneously. In his mobile headquarters he worked out the most original and unorthodox tactics for which there was no precedent in military history. He now rose to his full height not only as an inspirer of men in danger, tapping the innnermost moral resources of the revolution, but as a commander, manager and organizer. His moral and physical courage, with which he infected those who were weakening in their resolve, was seemingly inexhaustible. As in the heady days of October, he became a hero of the embattled multitudes.

In March 1919 Trotsky made a brief appearance, in

The main fronts in the civil war and war of intervention, 1919–20.
Under Trotsky's military leadership the young Soviet state defeated the armies of fifteen nations.

military uniform, at the founding Congress of the Third International. He presented the delegates with a stirring manifesto and a call to revolution. 'Today Moscow is the centre of the Third International. Tomorrow — this is our profound conviction — the centre will shift westwards, to Berlin, to Paris, to London … What happiness it is to live and fight in such times!', he exclaimed, and returned to the front.

However, the great prospects and the hopes that soon revolutionary Europe would rise and, as Lenin said, 'take Russia in tow', had gone to the wind. The first workers' state lay prostrate, utterly ruined by years of war, civil war and intervention. The proletarian dictatorship was triumphant, but the proletariat had nearly vanished. As a social class it had never been numerous. Now, in the ravaged country with industry destroyed or at a standstill, with no jobs, demoralized by idleness, by the black market and the sheer struggle for survival, it had disintegrated.

'At the very pinnacle of power Trotsky, like the protagonist of a classical tragedy, stumbled,' says Isaac Deutscher describing Trotsky's 'Defeat in Victory'.

Towards the end of the bloody and prolonged civil strife the ruling party was faced with the task of carrying the country from war to peace. And here Trotsky initiated a series of actions which were contrary to his own principles and which could be implemented only through breaking the resistance of the social classes which made or supported the revolution. Workers' detachments were sent to the countryside to requisition food. But the peasant would produce no more than he needed for himself and his family. He had no incentive to sell. He could not buy anything with the devalued roubles which he was offered for his produce. There was nothing to buy anyhow: there were no raw materials; the machinery was destroyed or rusty; the workers had fled to the countryside in search of food or to find jobs for which they could be paid in kind. The towns were famished and the countryside sullen and hostile. When the countryside refuses to produce food for the town, even the rudiments of urban civilization go to pieces.

If the workers cannot be brought back to the factory bench with the promise of better living, they have to be forced back. This was the logic which led to the militarization of labour and the policy of war communism; and nobody was more insistent and more outspoken in defence of that policy than Trotsky. If the revolution had sent thousands to die on the battlefields of civil war, had it not the moral right — nay, the duty — to send people into workshops and mines where the battle for survival must be waged? We 'must cultivate the spirit of the worker in the soldier and preserve the soldier in the worker … A deserter from labour is as contemptible and despicable as a deserter from the battlefield. Severe punishment to both!' — thus he addressed the newly formed labour battalions. But this time even his most brilliant rhetorical style could find only a faint echo in conscripted workers.

The country was in the grip of a mortal illness. The disillusionment was changing into bitterness, the discontent into despair, the despair into disturbances, the disturbances into revolt.

In March 1921 the sailors of Kronstadt, dominated by anarchists, formed a 'revolutionary' committee which assumed power in the city and put forward their demands for new elections to the Soviet, for the legalization of other parties, for the restoration of free trade and cancellation of other restrictive measures. The insurgents had in their hands heavy artillery, mortars and machine guns, and their fortress dominated the approaches to Petrograd. They could easily be exploited by the White Guards and other counter-revolutionary elements who, not without reason, saw in their action a threat to Soviet power. Soon the cry 'Down with Bolshevik tyranny' resounded throughout Kronstadt. The Bolshevik commanders on the spot were demoted and imprisoned. On 5 March Trotsky ordered the rebels to surrender unconditionally. 'Only those who do so', he warned, 'can count on the mercy of the Soviet Republic.' At the same time he announced his readiness to suppress the mutiny by force of arms. On 8 March a half-hearted offensive against Kronstadt began; it was repulsed. For another week the military operations were suspended. The insurrectionists increased their forces with an influx of deserters and elements hostile to the revolution. Finally, the order was given for a frontal assault. White sheets over their uniforms, the Bolshevik troops under Tukhachevsky's command advanced across the frozen Bay of Finland. The hurricane of fire melted the glassy surface under their feet. Wave upon wave of soldiers disappeared in the icy vortex. Fresh columns moved forward. On 17 March the attackers managed to scale the walls of the fortress. The rebels were defeated, but the triumph of the victors had a taste as bitter as hemlock.

Subsequently, the Kronstadt episode acquired an importance and a symbolism quite out of proportion to the actual event. Risings of a similar character had occurred in other provinces. But in the hands of the insurgents Kronstadt, as a fortress dominating the Baltic coast, presented the new republic with a formidable threat. Were the rebellion not suppressed in time, it might have been used, by foes within and without, as the spark to ignite anew the fires of the civil war. The tragedy of Kronstadt lay in the fact that the pure revolutionary idealism of some rebels was swamped by hostile forces and exploited for their own sinister ends. There was more sadness than exultation in Trotsky's 'victory speech': 'We waited as long as possible for our blinded sailor-comrades to see with their own eyes where the mutiny led ... '

To Lenin the Kronstadt events were 'like a flash of lightning which threw more glare on reality than anything else'. And the reality was grim. It became obvious that the revolution had to retreat. Even before the thunder and lightning of Kronstadt the party had embarked on a New Economic Policy; it abandoned the militarization of labour, it allowed a greater measure of free trade and introduced more private initiative in the countryside and in the towns. The urban bourgeoisie and the individualistic peasantry, having acquired more scope in pursuing their interests, were naturally seeking to create their own organs of political expression. This the ruling party was determined to prevent. Thus, paradoxically, 'liberalization' was followed by the tightening of the political régime and a ban on parties wishing to take advantage of that 'liberalization'. And so, not without misgivings, the party established its own monopoly of political power.

Thus it came to pass that the party substituted itself for the working class which, engulfed by the sheer struggle for survival, became incapable of asserting itself and managing its affairs; then the Central Committee substituted itself for the party; the single dictator was already mustering his myrmidons. Surreptitiously, slowly, slyly and with ostentatious modesty, Stalin, as the General Secretary of the Central Committee, was climbing all the rungs of command.

Lenin remembered the dreadful winter of 1920–21 as one during which the country and the party were consumed by 'mortal illness'. Soon, all too soon, he himself became the victim of a mortal illness. Towards the end of his life he felt that 'powerful forces were diverting the Soviet state from its proper road'. On his death-bed he made a last effort and warned the party that Stalin had been allowed to gather too much power in his hands and advised his followers to 'remove' him. But by that time Stalin had gathered so much power that he could suppress Lenin's testament.

It has often been said that Trotsky's nerve snapped and that in the struggle for the succession he committed one error after another and facilitated Stalin's ultimate victory. Hindsight indeed makes his behaviour — somewhat inert, contemptuous and haughty — appear foolish. It was true that Lenin's death, at the moment of the closest agreement and understanding between the two men, plunged Trotsky into numb despair; it was true that he was too proud to engage in undignified in-trigues over Lenin's coffin; it was true that he viewed the sly and scheming General Secretary with contempt and could not admit, even to himself, that this man could be his rival. It may be true that he kept aloof and silent when he should have spoken; it may be true that he failed to act when he should have acted. In the early days, when the mediocre Stalin fought against his great opponent with nothing more than preposterous calumny, he made a shrewd remark: Trotsky's strength, he said, reveals itself when the revolution gains momentum and advances; his weakness comes to the fore when the revolution is defeated and must retreat. The heroic phase of the revolution was coming to an end. The bureaucrats, not the revolutionary fighters, were taking over. The arch-bureaucrat Stalin had been patiently weaving his net of intrigues, making sure that as many posts as possible were filled with his supporters, with people who thought like him or who were content to leave it to him to do the thinking. He furthered their careers and their gratitude helped him to reinforce his own position. Gradually, almost imperceptibly, the huge 'apparatus', the whole machinery of power, was at his command.

Trotsky resigned from the Commissariat of War in 1925. During a lull in the inner-party struggle he wrote on Literature and Revolution, on Europe and America, on Problems of Everyday Life. In 1926 he tried to ally himself with Zinoviev and Kamenev against Stalin. But both, having previously supported Stalin in the short-lived Triumvirate, were now, when Stalin had turned against them, demoralized, vacillating and weak. Some two years later Zinoviev and Kamenev attempted again to counteract Stalin's inexorable rise. They approached Bukharin who, like themselves, had previously helped Stalin to defeat Trotsky. But Bukharin was now broken in spirit and paralysed with fear. Without even daring to pronounce Stalin's name, he repeated obsessively: 'He will slay us,' 'He is the new Genghis Khan,' 'He will strangle us.' In less than a decade the prophecy came true.

In the year in which the revolution celebrated the tenth anniversary of its victory, Trotsky — the architect of that victory — was expelled from the Bolshevik Party. A few months later he was exiled to Alma Alta, on the Russo-Chinese border. Those of his followers who unlike Zinoviev, Kamenev and Bukharin refused to bow to Stalin's blackmail and recant their views, were also exiled from Moscow. Stalin had learned his lessons in conspiracy from Tsarist times: he was careful to scatter his opponents far and wide so as to make their contacts almost impossible. Rakovsky was deported to Astrakhan, Radek to Tobolsk, Preobrazhensky to Uralsk, Smilga to Narym, Beloborodov to Ust-Kylom (Komi); others to Semi-Palatinsk in Central Asia, to

Tara, to Novo-Bayazet (Armenia), to Voronezh, Barnaul, Kaminsk, Minussinsk, Aktyubinsk, Tashkent, Kolpashevo. Isolated, gagged, vilified, yet displaying prodigious energy and stamina, Trotsky still managed to keep in touch with his adherents. But even these tenuous links seemed too dangerous to Stalin. In 1929 Trotsky, Natalya and Lyova were deported to a place altogether more remote — to Turkey. Prinkipo Island, in the Sea of Marmara, was their 'home' for four years. Innumerable attempts at moving closer to Europe were thwarted. No government, no matter how 'democratic', would offer Trotsky asylum for any length of time.

The truth was that even disarmed and alone Trotsky inspired fear in all established governments and ruling parties. Churchill called him mockingly 'The Ogre of Europe', triumphing over the enemy once so powerful, who now 'sits disconsolate, a bundle of old rags, stranded on the shores of the Black Sea'. George Bernard Shaw looked deeper and saw more clearly. He derided his Labour Party friends, then in power under Ramsay MacDonald, for having 'an unreasoning dread of him as a caged lion ... If the government by excluding Mr Trotsky could also have silenced him ... But Mr Trotsky cannot be silenced ... He becomes the inspirer and the hero of all the militants of the extreme left of every country.'

All through his enforced peregrinations Trotsky never remained silent for longer than it took him to unpack his papers and seize his pen. With only Lyova, who never wavered in his devotion to his father's cause, as assistant and helpmeet, and a small handful of transient foreign sympathizers, he instantly reacted to, and commented on, every event of contemporary politics: on the rise of fascism, on Roosevelt's New Deal, on the Spanish Civil War, and above all on the social disease of Nazism. He provided incisive analyses of developments, political and economic, in his own country and increasingly denounced Stalin's misdeeds.

Some of the places of exile to which Trotskyists were dispersed after 1927 to hinder political contact between them. Despite the difficulties, they maintained communications for some years.

These were the years when Stalin, after having silenced and eliminated his critics and rivals, embarked upon policies infinitely more drastic and cruel than any that Trotsky had advocated in the immediate aftermath of the civil war. He plunged Russia into a kind of 'second revolution': a frenetic process of forced collectivization of farming and a no less forced and extra-rapid industrialization of the country.

When the peasants, who themselves were living at starvation level, refused to part with their meagre products, they were faced with military squads. Those who were against their will incorporated into collective and state farms established by decree preferred to slaughter their cattle and smash their implements rather than bring them into the new 'kolkhozy'. Those who refused to enter the collectives had to leave their homesteads, were rounded up and deported to remote regions of Siberia. 'Collectivization' degenerated into a bloody military operation. Vast tracts of land remained untilled. Famine stalked the towns as well as the most fertile regions of the Ukraine, the granary of Russia.

This tour de force in the countryside was followed by a tour de force in industry which, in the first instance, had to produce agricultural machinery. It was now a matter of life and death that the tractor should replace the horse and the wooden plough. For this a new industrial base had to be built: new oil wells, new coal mines, new steel plants, new power stations. In a word: The Soviet Union had to move or be precipitated into the twentieth century.

Manpower was not lacking. Thousands and thousands of young peasants were running away from the embattled villages; but they had neither the skill nor the discipline of urbanized workers. Herded into overcrowded and hastily constructed barracks, formed into work battalions, they were subjected to a draconian labour code: the slightest insubordination was punished with deportation; bewildered by the machinery which he had never handled in his life, a benighted peasant who happened to damage a tool was seen as a 'saboteur' and 'wrecker' and promptly dispatched to a camp for 're-education'. He was thus joining other 'saboteurs': recalcitrant peasants, dissenters, critics, members of religious sects or just malcontents. 'Re-education' became slave labour, cruel, wasteful of human life, a huge black sprawling stain on the grim enough picture of the country.

In the process of that frenetic 'second revolution' which claimed millions of victims, Stalin had no scruple in jettisoning the ideals in the name of which the October Revolution was made. The achievements of Peter the Great were being extolled, while Lenin, robbed of his true substance, became a harmless icon. There was no more talk about internationalism. 'Socialism in One

Country', Stalin's reply to Trotsky's theory of Permanent Revolution, became the ruling doctrine. Hurt by the lack of support of the western proletariat, Russia withdrew into her national shell and was being fed the most blatant nationalistic slogans. There was no more talk about equality: incentives, piecework, competitiveness, wage differentials, privileges became the order of the day. The old socialist dream about proletarian democracy and self-determination of the working class, about the freedom of organization and expression might have lingered on. But the 'organization' was ruthlessly imposed from above and freedom of expression reserved for those who praised The Leader. The 'cult of personality' — the adulation of the 'Father of the People' — reached ridiculous, byzantine proportions. 'The Shining Sun of Humanity' was leading his people to the socialist paradise. Those who did not spontaneously believe were made to believe by force. The truth was that Stalin's socialism was being built by coercion and not by persuasion. No leader could admit this. And so truth was banished from the country which had aspired to become the first workers' state, but turned instead into the country of The Great Lie, 'Le Pays du Grand Mensonge' in the words of Anton Ciliga, a now forgotten old revolutionary.

Coercion, repression, persecution and terror were spreading all over Russia in ever-widening circles.

In 1936–8 Stalin staged his 'Moscow Trials', which in their perversity had no parallel in history. Since Trotsky's expulsion from the Soviet Union, the immense resources of Stalin's propaganda machine were harnessed to the struggle against the Great Exile. 'Trotskyism' became a term of abuse, an offence deserving the supreme punishment. Trotsky was portrayed as the enemy of the people, the traitor to his country who conspired with Hitler and the Mikado and aimed at the dismemberment of the Soviet Union, as the incarnation of the Devil who threatened Stalin's paradise. The nightmarish campaign reached its climax when, on 15 August 1936, Moscow announced that a trial of the 'Trotskyite-Zinovievite Terrorist Centre' was about to open. This was the first of the series of infamous trials in which nearly all the leaders of the October Revolution, members of Lenin's Politbureau, many outstanding scientists and writers and most commanders of the Red Army were denounced as traitors and foreign spies, and executed. The trials succeeded each other until 1938, though this was not the end of the purges, which became a feature of Stalin's rule until his death.

Although Stalin himself never appeared in the courtroom, he was the author, the producer and prompter of the chilling spectacle. The nightmarish quality of the 'trials' was heightened by the perversity of the accusations and the performance of the defendants in the dock: the heroic figures of the revolution were all made to 'confess' to crimes which they could not have committed; they were denied every possibility to defend themselves; they were plunged into the abyss of humiliation and not allowed even to die in dignity. The 'proceedings' reached their bizarre culmination with the ranting of the chief prosecutor Vyshinsky, who demanded that all the accused be 'shot like mad dogs'. Trotsky, the chief actor in this hallucinatory stage play, was sentenced to death in absentia.

He was outside Stalin's absolutist republic, and yet he was unable to refute the flood of abuse and denunciations from Moscow. He was gagged not by Stalin's acolytes, but by the Social Democratic government of Norway which had granted him the right of asylum in 1935. At first he was received with honours. But after less than a year the Socialist Minister of Justice, Trygve Lie (the future Secretary-General of the United Nations), somehow 'suspended' his liberal socialist convictions and obtained, by royal decree, the right to intern the illustrious exile. Confined to house arrest and held incommunicado, Trotsky was kept under strict police guard. By a quirk of fate the officer in charge of the internee was Jonas Lie, the future chief of police in the wartime government of Major Quisling, the eponymous Norwegian traitor.

It was not until the spring of the following year that Trotsky was able to raise his voice in denunciation of Stalin's macabre forgeries. Expelled from Norway and sent in great secrecy in a ramshackle boat across the ocean, he found refuge in Mexico. With superhuman energy he set out to organize his defence.

In April 1937 a Commission of Inquiry under the presidency of the American philosopher John Dewey began to sift the evidence and to cross-examine the chief defendant of Stalinist 'justice'. The investigation conducted by the commission was thorough: no questions were left unanswered, no issues blurred, and no relevant historical incidents remained unclarified. The great authority of John Dewey, his integrity and detachment from all political strife, guaranteed the impartiality of the findings. After long deliberations the Dewey Commission concluded its work and pronounced its verdict: 'Not guilty'. The report, published in two bulky volumes, 'The Case of Leon Trotsky' and 'Not Guilty', substantiated the verdict to the full.

What should have been the resounding voice of truth and justice was, however, muffled by other sounds and the blaring of powerful propaganda machines. Among the radical and leftist intelligentsia, mesmerized by Stalin's power, very few were prepared to shed their comfortable illusions about the purity of the Workers'

Fatherland; the established bourgeois governments and their supporters derived some satisfaction from what they saw as the fratricidal strife between two equally hateful revolutionaries. Others had their gaze fixed on the darkening horizon over Europe threatened by the terrible scourge of Nazism and world war which was looming ahead.

Not a word of the counter-trial reached the Soviet people. Stalin seemed invulnerable and all-powerful. And yet he could not but sense resentments all around him. The peasantry had not recovered from the shocks of forcible collectivization; the town-dwellers had not forgotten the years of famine and terror. The purges decimated the intelligentsia: few were the families in which one or more members had not disappeared into the vast wilderness of Siberia or perished in the dark caves of some prison. And the world was on the brink of Armaggedon.

In August 1939 Stalin signed a pact with Hitler, trying to deflect the enormous Nazi war machine to the West. Trotsky — the lonely exile in far-away Mexico — was tirelessly denouncing Stalin's crimes and especially his collusion with Hitler, a crime of which he had so grotesquely accused the victims of the purges.

Stalin was more than ever impatient to stifle this voice. On 24 May 1940 in the dead of night a gang of armed Mexican Stalinists carried out an attempt on Trotsky's life. The attempt failed. The next one was better prepared — and successful.

A GPU agent had unobtrusively wormed his way into Trotsky's entourage. Posing as a faithful disciple, he pretended to seek the Master's opinion on a piece of writing. When Trotsky, sitting at the desk, was bent over the manuscript, the man delivered one powerful and well-aimed blow. An ice-axe split Trotsky's skull. Mortally wounded, he still jumped at the murderer, threw at him whatever object was to hand, and fought like a tiger until, covered with blood, he finally collapsed into the arms of his wife and his guards who ran in at the sound of the struggle.

Thus the death sentence was carried out on the man condemned in absentia by the Moscow 'tribunal'. The weapon was wielded by an obscure agent named variously as 'Mercader' or 'Jacson' or 'Mornard', but the executioner was immured in the Kremlin, thousands of miles away.

On 21 August 1940 Trotsky's life, divided from his early years 'not only in space and time by decades and by far countries, but by the mountain chain of great events', came to an end in a suburb of Mexico. He was buried in the garden of the Coyoacan villa which had been fortified in a vain attempt to bar hostile intruders. A white rectangular stone marked with a hammer and sickle was raised above the grave.

Natalya, his devoted wife and companion, was to live on in the house for over twenty years. Immersed in her grief, she was like the legendary Niobe: a martyred mother mourning not only her husband but the cruel death of all their children.

When in 1926, in the heat of the conflict, Trotsky had assailed Stalin, calling him 'the grave-digger of the revolution', another old Bolshevik, shaken and terrified, exclaimed: 'Why did you say this? Stalin will never forgive you, not until the third or the fourth generation.' The prediction was dramatically fulfilled: Trotsky's first wife, Sokolovskaya, died in Siberian exile; their two daughters, Nina and Zina, were driven to death by Stalin; their husbands perished in deportation. Lyova, Trotsky's and Natalya's first born, who was his father's most devoted assistant and shared all the bitterness of exile, died in Paris in mysterious circumstances; Sergei, their younger son, a scientist uninvolved in political work, stayed on in the Soviet Union, and he too became the victim of Stalin's vengeance. The wives and children of both disappeared without a trace.

Only Zina's son, Vsevolod, remained alive. He and his family are now lovingly tending the trees, shrubs and ever-blossoming flowers around the austere white stone in the garden — the graveyard — of the house which from a refuge turned into a death trap.

What is the heritage of Trotsky and what is the relevance of his work for our time?

Trotsky remained all his life an indomitable fighter and revolutionary, but even had his activities been on a smaller scale, he would still be classed as an outstanding thinker and Marxist theorist.

The theory of Permanent Revolution is his distinctive contribution to the body of Marxist thought. He first formulated and published it in 1906, as we have seen, under the title 'Results and Prospects'. He viewed the transition from capitalism to socialism not as one final act, but as a series of interdependent and interconnected social upheavals occurring in countries of diverse social structures and on various levels of civilization. No single phase of this process was self-contained or self-sufficient; it was a chain reaction in which every new impulse set others in motion. (The awakening of national and social consciousness which finds its expression in national liberation movements among the peoples of Asia and Africa may be interpreted as a confirmation of the permanency of the revolution.) In the Europe-dominated world of stable empires and dynasties of Trotsky's youth, this was a bold and original conception.

Most Marxists of his time maintained that any attempt at socialist revolution had to take place in the developed West and that Russia could at best strive only to abolish her feudalism and transform herself into a modern capitalist state. Trotsky, on the contrary, had the vision of an upheaval that would begin by taking Russia towards a bourgeois society, but in the process would develop further and deeper in the direction of a proletarian régime.

Up to 1914 the difference between the Mensheviks and the Bolsheviks consisted precisely in this, that the former saw bourgeois democracy as the goal of the revolution and wanted the workers to lend their support to the middle classes who were to lead it, while the latter saw the middle classes as too timid and too ready to compromise with Tsardom to be able to lead anywhere. Only the workers, the Bolsheviks maintained, allied with the peasantry were bold enough to lead a determined struggle against autocracy. But, Trotsky had argued, if the industrial working classes were to act as the vanguard of the revolution, the revolution's own momentum and logic would lead to the establishment of a proletarian, not a bourgeois, democracy.

Classical Marxism was entirely based on the assumption that a socialist revolution would take place in an advanced society, at a high level of technological development, amidst an abundance of goods and services. Russia, at the beginning of the century, presented a totally different picture; therefore, in Trotsky's scheme of things, Russia could only begin to build socialism but could not complete it otherwise than with the help of the industrial proletariat of the West. No revolution could be a self-contained national event; it had to cross and re-cross frontiers and become 'permanent' in the geographical sense too. To Trotsky permanent revolution was an organic historic process and he was firmly opposed to any action of minorities unsupported by the mass of the workers. He spoke as strongly against local coups as against 'carrying the revolution on the point of bayonets' of 'friendly armies'. The doctrine of 'Socialism in One Country', elaborated by Stalin, was to be the answer to Trotsky's Permanent Revolution. It led to Soviet isolationism, self-sufficiency, nationalism and the subordination of every communist principle to Soviet raison d'état.

Among Trotsky's prolific comments on events leading to the Second World War the most important was his analysis of national socialism. While Moscow belittled the danger of Nazism and, with sham radicalism, treated Social Democracy and Fascism as 'twins', Trotsky made desperate efforts to arouse the German workers, and indeed the whole world, to the mortal peril. He advocated a 'united front' between Communists and Socialists, which alone could stem the rising tide of Hitler's battalions.

Trotsky's critique of Soviet bureaucracy is another subject which has lost nothing of its topicality. Whether Soviet bureaucracy is a 'new class' or a new 'stratum', whether it should be abolished by reform or by revolution is still hotly debated in various Marxist circles. To the end Trotsky maintained that the Soviet Union, even under Stalin, was a 'workers' state', though a 'degenerate' one, where some premises of socialism have been laid, and that it was still the duty of socialists to defend it unconditionally against imperialist attack.

In evaluating Trotsky's life and work, his talents as a writer cannot be forgotten. His 'History of the Russian Revolution' has been recognized as a masterpiece by friend and foe alike. Literary criticism, military and journalistic comment, and social analysis flowed from his pen and filled many volumes.

He was defeated in his lifetime, accused of heinous crimes, and eventually murdered. His works are still banned from his own country, the country he had so actively helped to build. They are banned from China and all other countries in which the Soviet model of socialism prevails. The Fourth International, which he set up in 1938, has not proved effective as an instrument of revolution, but it has played a considerable role as a stimulus to world-wide debate on the basic tenets of Trotskyism and to the creation of numerous groups searching for a correct revolutionary strategy for our time. Since the 1960s Trotsky's own writings have achieved widespread popularity — and sales — far greater than in his lifetime.

Whenever class struggle intensifies and the ruling classes are haunted by the spectre of revolution, one of the names they give that spectre is 'Trotskyism'.

Nearly half a century after his death, the same 'unreasoning dread' of Trotsky which Bernard Shaw had detected in Ramsay MacDonald's Labour Party still persists whether the party is in or out of office. To the satisfaction, and amusement, of those who hold power in London and Moscow, some of MacDonald's successors call for a witchhunt against Trotskyist influences in their party. And as Shaw predicted: even silenced, Trotsky became 'the inspirer and the hero of all the militants of the extreme left of every country'.

Tamara Deutscher
London, 1986

This narrative of Trotsky's life is based entirely on Isaac Deutscher's three-volume biography 'The Prophet Armed', 'The Prophet Unarmed' and 'The Prophet Outcast', published by Oxford University Press.

RUSSIA, EUROPE, AMERICA 1879-1917

FROM YANOVKA TO THE FINLAND STATION

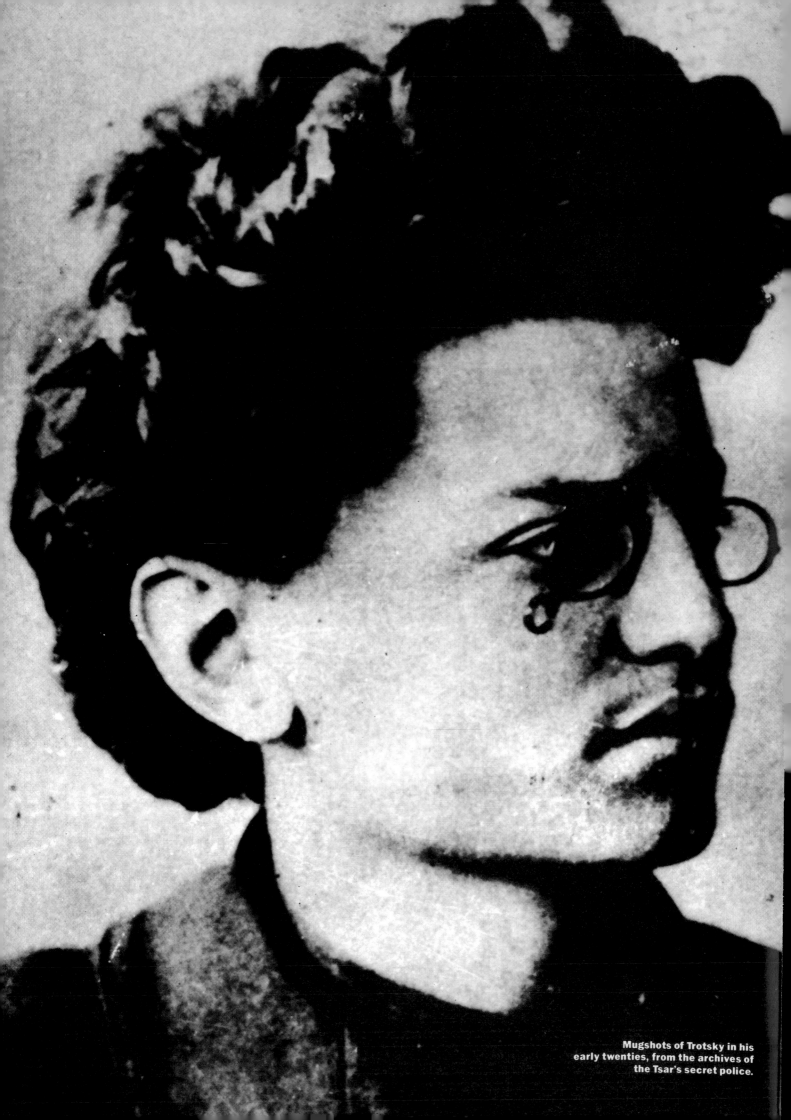

Mugshots of Trotsky in his early twenties, from the archives of the Tsar's secret police.

In 1879, the year of Trotsky's birth, his parents had moved with their family to a 750-acre farm in Yanovka, a village on the vast steppes of the Southern Ukraine. Their first dwelling was modest, a peasants' house of mud walls and a leaky straw roof. But David Bronstein was a frontiersman, tough and ambitious, determined to improve his position by means of thrift and hard work — his own, his wife's and his labourers'. His treatment of seasonal workers sometimes drew protests. Trotsky later recalled: 'The labourers would leave the fields and collect in the courtyard. They would lie face downward in the shade of the barns, brandishing their bare, cracked, straw-pricked feet in the air, and wait to see what would happen. Then my father would give them some sour milk, or water-melons, or half a

sack of dried fish, and they would go back to work again, often singing. These were the conditions on all the farms.'

The year of Trotsky's birth was also the year of the first terrorist attacks against Tsarism. But the explosions of dynamite thrown by the Narodniks (Populists) found no echo in South Russia, 'a kingdom of wheat and sheep, living by laws all its own . . . firmly guarded against the invasion of politics by its great open spaces and the absence of roads'.

Above: Agricultural labourers photographed in the Ukraine towards the end of the nineteenth century.

The old man had plans for his son Lev Davidovich. The child was obviously very bright, and the farm would soon need an engineer to build a sugar-mill and a brewery. So the nine-year-old was sent to a good school in Odessa.

He lived with his uncle and aunt, the Schpentzers, cultured, elegant and kindly people. They taught him good manners and introduced him to literature and the theatre. 'I was becoming a little urbanite. Occasionally, however, the village would flare up in my consciousness and draw me on like a lost paradise. Then I would pine, wander about, and trace with my finger on the window-pane messages to my mother, or I would cry into my pillow.'

At school he soon came top of his class, showing a particular interest in history. He read feverishly, finding in the answer to one question the germs of several more. He showed no aptitude for sports.

It was discovered that he was short-sighted, and he was prescribed spectacles. 'This did not hurt my pride at all, for the glasses gave me a sense of added importance. For my father, however, the glasses were a great blow. He held that it was affectation and swank on my part, and peremptorily demanded that I remove them ... In Yanovka I wore the glasses only secretly.' He clashed with the school authorities, too, and was twice expelled for organizing protests against unfair treatment. But he was soon reinstated, for his teachers considered him 'the pride of the school'.

Marxists were active in Odessa then, but the young Bronstein was unaware of them. When in the summer of 1896 he moved to Nikolayev to complete his secondary education, he was the picture of a little bourgeois, dapper and self-assured. He showed no interest in politics, imagining for himself a brilliant career in mathematics. His landlady offered him as an example to her sons, who were attracted by the ideas of socialism. Inwardly, however, he was having greater difficulty making sense of the world and of his place in it than his behaviour suggested.

Above left: Anna Bronstein came from urban middle-class stock and only gradually accustomed herself to village life. Unusually for a Jewish woman of the time, she could read a little Russian. She was not demonstratively affectionate, but she shared a strong comradeship of labour with her husband.

Left: David Leontievich Bronstein was one of a rare breed, the Jewish farmer. At 60 he taught himself the Russian alphabet so that he could at least make out the titles of his son's books. He was ruined by the revolution but reconciled himself with it. He died aged 83, the successful manager of a state mill.

Opposite page: Trotsky at the age of nine. He was handsome, polite, very clever — and proud of it. According to his aunt, Fanny Schpentzer, 'The worst trouble I had was that he was so terribly neat. I remember once he had a new suit and we went out walking, and all the way he kept picking imaginary lint off that suit ... He had to have everything perfect.'

32

Abruptly the seventeen-year-old abandoned his worldly-wise dismissal of 'socialistic utopias' for the passionate embrace of revolution. He was attracted by the romanticism of the Narodniks. A market gardener named Shvigovsky had gathered around him a group of bohemians, and in their company Bronstein neglected his studies for dangerous conversation. Soon they organized a society for the distribution of 'useful books' among the people.

Among the group was Alexandra Sokolovskaya, a Marxist. The young men fell in love with her, and loved to scoff at her politics. Bronstein organized practical jokes at her

expense, and she refused to speak to him. But he underwent another sudden conversion and with her founded the 'South Russian Workers' Union'. In the spring of 1897 huge strikes erupted in St Petersburg, led by Lenin. Bronstein and his friends set out to organize the workers of Nikolayev. By the end of the year their group had over 200 members. But early in 1898 they were arrested. Bronstein spent two and a half years in solitary confinement before being sentenced without trial to four years' exile in Siberia. He and Alexandra were married in jail, ensuring that they spent their years of deportation together.

Above: Alexandra Sokolovskaya with her brother Grigory on her right and Lev Davidovich on her left. At her feet is G. Ziv, a medical student. Together with a mechanic by the name of Ivan Andreyevich Mukhin, this group formed the core of the South Russian Workers' Union, the first social-democratic (i.e. revolutionary) organization in Nikolayev. Arrested with the others in 1898, Ziv later became a political opponent of Trotsky's, emigrated to the USA, and wrote in 1921 a poisonous little memoir of their days in Nikolayev.
Opposite page: L. D., alias Lvov, in 1897.

Deportees, autumn 1900:
Alexandra is in the front row on the right,
L.D. seated by her right shoulder.

The years in jail and exile were not wasted. In Odessa Lev Davidovich taught himself some French, German, Italian and English through reading translations of the Bible. Later he acquired some tomes of Hegelian-Marxist philosophy, and set about constructing for himself a coherent revolutionary outlook.

In Siberia he began his career as a writer, contributing articles to local papers on many subjects, especially literary criticism. He studied Marx's 'Das Kapital' in depth. He threw himself into the debates then raging among the exiles about 'legal' versus revolutionary Marxism, and Marxism versus anarchism. Among the revolutionary Marxists there were disagreements on the form their party should take: federalist or centralized? Bronstein (alias Antid Oto, Italian for antidote) aroused controversy for his strong advocacy of a dominant Central Committee.

In summer 1902 he received a copy of Lenin's 'What is to be done?' and back numbers of 'Iskra' ('The Spark'), the paper Lenin, Plekhanov and others published abroad. Bronstein found there an extended statement of his own ideas. Suddenly Siberia seemed stiflingly parochial. He agreed with Alexandra that he should attempt an escape. Leaving a dummy in his bed, he travelled under bales of hay in a peasant cart to Irkutsk. There comrades gave him a faked passport, in which he inscribed the name of one of his jailers in Odessa — Trotsky. He boarded the Trans-Siberian Railway for Samara. Shortly after his arrival there came a message from Lenin: the young writer was to join him in London. He knocked on the door of 30 Holford Square, Kings Cross, at dawn one morning in October 1902.

Top left: Trotsky in Siberia.
Top right: Alexandra with other political exiles after Trotsky's escape.
Above left: Alexandra (third from left) holding her and Trotsky's second daughter, Nina, late 1902. The woman on the right is holding the couple's first child, Zina (Zinaida).
Above right: Trotsky, nicknamed in those days Piero (The Pen), pictured shortly after his arrival in western Europe.
Opposite page: The couple before Trotsky's escape in late summer 1902.

Winter in Siberia, 1901–2: Alexandra and Zina are on the right, Trotsky fourth from the left.

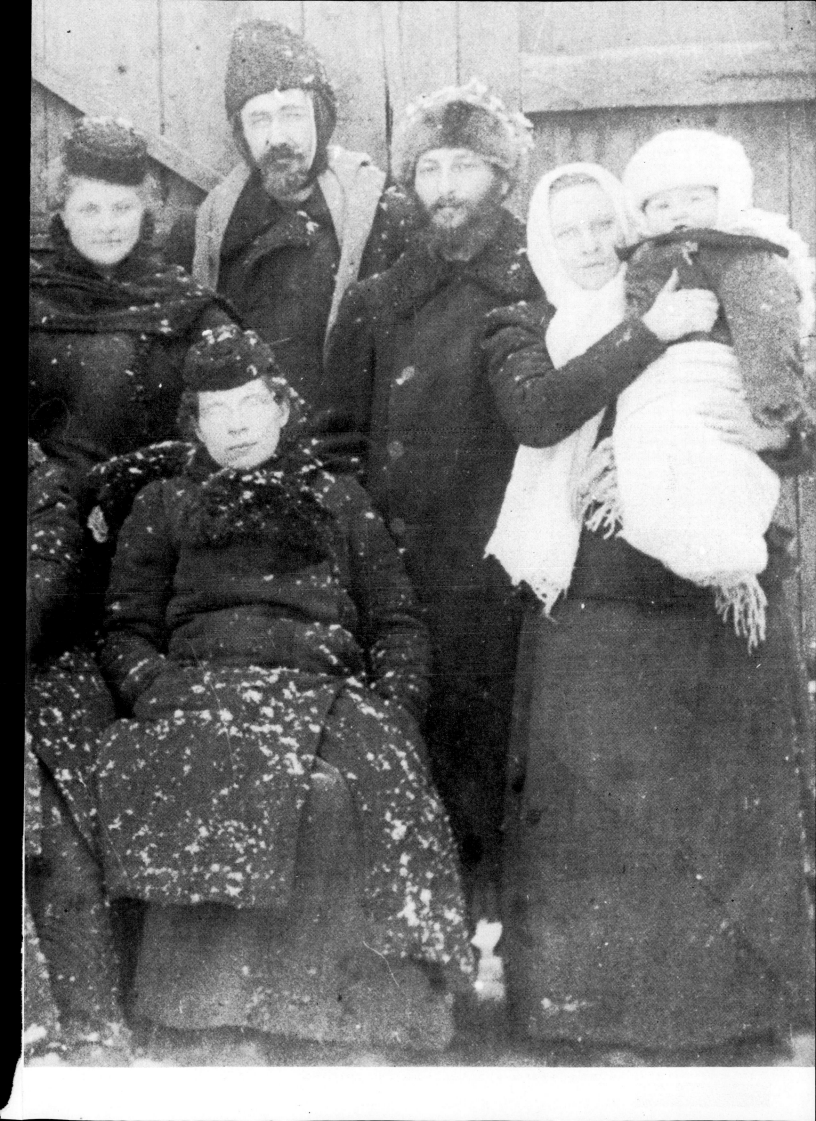

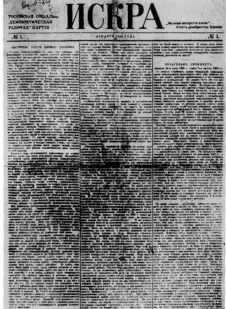

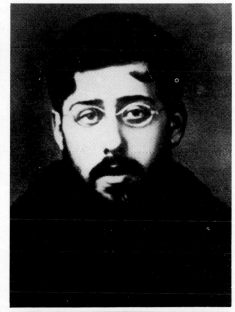

Top left: Nadezhada Krupskaya, organizer of contacts between the exiles and the Russian underground; wife of Lenin.
Top centre: Issue 1 of 'Iskra' ('The Spark'), motto: 'The spark will kindle a flame.'
Top right: Georgi Plekhanov, theoretician and forerunner of Russian Marxism.
Above left: Vera Zasulich. In 1878 she shot the hated General Trepov, was acquitted by the jury and escaped abroad. The Tsar subsequently abolished juries for political trials. Zasulich helped found the Russian Marxist party.
Above centre: Yulii Martov.
Above right: Pavel Axelrod. When Trotsky met him, he lived in Zurich and earned his living by making buttermilk.
Opposite page: Vladimir Ilyich Ulyanov, known as Lenin.

Now barely twenty-three, Trotsky found himself in the company of the giants of Russian Marxism. Lenin took him on a guided tour of London while his wife Krupskaya arranged a room in the house shared by Vera Zasulich and Yulii Martov, two members of the 'Iskra' editorial board.

'Iskra' was controlled by a coalition of two groups. The older generation, led by Zasulich, Georgi Plekhanov and Pavel Axelrod, were veterans of the Emancipation of Labour group, formed in 1883. They had participated in the first attempt to form a united social-democratic (that is, revolutionary Marxist) party in 1898.

That project had failed as a result of drastic police action and, more seriously, an internal split. One faction, known as the 'Economists', took as their starting point the trade union movement and the fight for reforms; they objected to 'political dogmatism'; and they rejected the notion of a disciplined and centralized party. Plekhanov's faction asserted the primacy of politics over economic action and demanded that an all-Russia revolutionary party be built on scientific Marxist foundations.

Plekhanov's views on Economism were shared by the St Petersburg League of Struggle for the Emancipation of the Working Class, founded by Lenin, Martov and others in 1895. Zasulich made contact between the two groups, and the first issue of the joint publication 'Iskra' appeared in December 1900. The paper argued for a centralized revolutionary party, and itself organized some 100–150 members.

Trotsky was soon put to work writing articles (which were a little florid for Lenin's and Plekhanov's tastes) and lecturing in London, Brussels, Liège and Paris. During one Paris trip he met and fell in love with Natalya Sedova, a student Iskraite who had been given the task of finding him lodgings.

'Iskra' had an editorial board of six: three from the older group (Plekhanov, Zasulich and Axelrod) and three younger exiles (Lenin, Martov and Alexander Potresov). Voting on controversial questions was often tied. In order to break the deadlock Lenin presently proposed — unknown to Trotsky — that the newcomer become a seventh board member. Plekhanov took this proposal as a personal affront, and never forgave Trotsky for it. The plan was abandoned, but difficulties on the editorial board persisted.

Preparations were underway for the Second Congress of the Russian Social Democratic Workers' Party, to be held in Brussels in July 1903. The venue was the storeroom of a cooperative society, the Maison du Peuple. The room contained bales of wool, home to a vast army of fleas. Not the fleas, however, but the attentions of the Belgian police obliged the congress to adjourn to London in the middle of its business.

The first confrontation was with the Bundists (Jewish separatists); their demands were decisively rejected. Next the Economists were routed. These fights were expected, and Trotsky, who attended as a delegate from the Siberian Social Democratic Union, acquired the title 'Lenin's cudgel' for the aggression with which he spoke.

But what happened next hit Trotsky like a bolt from the blue: the 'Iskra' team tore itself apart before his eyes. Lenin and Martov proposed alternative clauses defining party membership. According to Lenin, a member was one who 'personally participates' in one of the Party's organizations; for Martov it was sufficient to 'cooperate personally and regularly under the guidance' of a Party organization. That there was a difference of opinion surprised no one: Lenin was generally considered a 'hard' man, and Martov 'soft'. Plekhanov among others considered the difference of small importance, but it led to a vicious row. Trotsky blamed Lenin for disruption, and sided with Martov, who won the vote.

Trotsky's suspicions were confirmed by a proposal from Lenin to reduce the editorial board of 'Iskra' to three — himself, Plekhanov and Martov. Not only was this rank discourtesy towards the other three members of the board; it looked like the crudest coup d'état against Martov, for Plekhanov was then Lenin's staunchest ally and Zasulich, Axelrod and Potresov sided with Martov. Trotsky moved a counterproposal, to confirm the existing membership of the board. But by this time the Bundists and Economists had walked out, and Lenin won by two votes. His followers were thereafter known as the Bolsheviks (the Majority), and Martov's supporters as the Mensheviks (the Minority). Martov immediately resigned from the board. Since a comparable political balance would prevail on the Party's Central Committee, the minority decided also to boycott these elections. Lenin's supporters were left in sole command, and the Party was split once more.

The row continued after the congress. Lenin soon lost control of 'Iskra' when Plekhanov deserted him. Trotsky wrote a muddled report of the congress to the Siberian Union, comparing Lenin with Robespierre, the Jacobin dictator of the French Revolution, and accusing him of 'bureaucratic centralism', 'will for power' and 'substitutionism'. At the same time he argued urgently for reunification of the party. Lenin called him a 'windbag'.

Trotsky could not grasp that a fundamental differentiation was taking place between revolutionary and reformist groupings. Political differences came ever more sharply into view, and on these points he generally agreed with the Bolsheviks — or stood to the left of them. But Lenin and his organization

42

he rejected, and he continued to do so for fourteen years. He soon belonged to neither faction, and his persistent attempts to bring them together were as futile as they were unpopular with both factions.

When 'Iskra' came under Menshevik control, Trotsky, now living in Geneva, resumed writing for it. But he soon clashed with his colleagues. They criticized him for the vehemence of his attacks on Lenin, and he became ever more worried about their softening attitude towards the liberals. In April 1904 Plekhanov succeeded in kicking him off the paper. He moved to Munich, where he was put up by Alexander Helphand, alias Parvus, another neither-Bolshevik-nor-Menshevik. Natalya Sedova later joined him.

Above: A demonstration in Moscow, 1905.
The first banner reads:
'Proletarians of all countries, unite!'
Left: Natalya Sedova in Munich, 1904.

In Russia there were rumblings of great events. Since 1900 the country had been in the grip of a severe economic crisis. In January 1904 Japan destroyed a large part of the Russian fleet in a surprise attack on Port Arthur. Reinforcements sent by the Tsar were annihilated in the Straits of Tsushima. Popular unrest was mounting rapidly. A revolutionary upheaval was clearly on the way, but what sort of revolution would this be?

The Mensheviks argued that Russia was economically backward and so would need to undergo a bourgeois revolution and an extended period of development before socialism was possible. The role of the workers' party, therefore, was to lend support to the liberals in a fight to create a democratic republic.

The Bolsheviks replied that the bourgeoisie was too weak and spineless to conduct a fight against the Tsar. While they did not disagree that the revolution would be basically bourgeois in character, they held that the working class would play the leading role. In this task they would seek and win the support of the peasantry.

Trotsky and Parvus were working on an altogether more radical theory when events interrupted the debate with their own reply. In December a major strike erupted in the oilfields of Baku. The workers won. On 3 January 1905 a strike broke out at the Putilov armaments factory in St Petersburg, the capital, and soon spread to other trades. On the 9th peaceful demonstrators were shot down outside the Tsar's palace, but the strike wave only grew.

Unencumbered with party responsibilities, Trotsky returned to Russia with Natalya in February. He took care to stay well underground, operating under a variety of assumed names. The strike wave was subsiding, but the workers were taking stock — and turning their ears to the message of the social-democratic agitators. None was more effective than Trotsky.

Throughout the summer sporadic strikes continued. Unrest spread to the countryside, where the peasants withheld taxes and took to looting large estates. In July sailors on the battleship 'Potemkin' mutinied at Odessa. But by now the police were on Trotsky's trail. Natalya had been arrested in May and jailed for six months, and in the summer he fled to Finland. There he passed a few weeks in a secluded pension named 'Rauha', meaning 'peace'. In the evenings the postman would bring the St Petersburg papers, brimming with news of fresh strikes. 'It was like a raging storm coming in through an open window ... In the silence of the hotel, the rustling of the papers echoed in one's ears like the rumble of an avalanche.'

The typesetters at Sytin's printworks in Moscow struck on 19 September. 'This small event set off nothing more nor less than the all-Russian political strike — the strike which started over punctuation marks and ended by felling absolutism.' Soon strikes enveloped the country from Finland to Siberia.

When Trotsky returned to St Petersburg on 15 October, the Soviet (Council) of Workers' Deputies was a few days old. He rapidly became its leader and thus the head of the first revolutionary workers' government in embryo. He was just twenty-six.

On 17 October, frightened by the general strike, the Tsar issued a manifesto promising a constitution — but meanwhile General Trepov (the man Zasulich had failed to kill) was giving his police the order to clear the streets: 'Spare no bullets!' Trotsky addressed a huge crowd:

'Citizens! Our strength is in ourselves. With sword in hand we must stand guard over our freedom. As for the Tsar's manifesto, look, it's only a scrap of paper. Here it is before you — here it is crumpled in my fist. Today they have issued it, tomorrow they will take it away and tear it into pieces, just as I am now tearing up this paper freedom before your eyes!'

The Bolsheviks denounced the Soviet as a distraction from building the party, and persisted in this attitude until Lenin's return to St Petersburg in November. Trotsky won the local Mensheviks to a revolutionary policy, and worked mostly with them. The Soviet declared itself for a republic — and then for a series of anti-capitalist demands including the eight-hour day. Finally they published a manifesto, written by Parvus, declaring a financial boycott of the Tsar.

But by now the régime had summoned the means, and the will, to counter-attack. On 3 December the Executive of the Soviet was arrested en masse. Troops were sent into the streets to crush all opposition.

43

'Death stalks the barricades',
a caricature by Boris Kustodiev depicting
the entry into Moscow
of the Semyonovsky regiment
in December 1905

In jail Trotsky had the opportunity to reflect on the events of 1905, and to complete the theoretical work which he and Parvus had begun in Munich. 'Results and Prospects', published while its author was incarcerated in the Peter-Paul Fortress, expounded the theory of permanent revolution.

'This rather high-flown expression', Trotsky wrote in a later summary, 'defines the thought that the Russian revolution, although directly concerned with bourgeois aims, could not stop short at those aims; the revolution could not solve its immediate, bourgeois tasks except by putting the proletariat into power. And the proletariat, once having power in its hands, would not be able to remain confined within the bourgeois framework of the revolution. On the contrary, precisely in order to guarantee its victory, the proletarian vanguard in the very earliest stages of its rule would have to make extremely deep inroads not only into feudal but also into bourgeois property relations. While doing so, it would enter into hostile conflict, not only with all those bourgeois groups which had supported it during the first stages of its revolutionary struggle, but also with the broad masses of the peasantry, with whose collaboration it had come into power.

'The contradictions between a workers' government and an overwhelming majority of peasants in a backward country could be resolved only on an international scale, in the arena of a world proletarian revolution. Having, by virtue of historical necessity, burst the narrow bourgeois-democratic confines of the Russian revolution, the victorious proletariat would be compelled also to burst its national and state confines, that is to say, it would have to strive consciously for the Russian revolution to become the prologue to a world revolution.'

Almost every copy of the book was seized by the police as soon as it was published. Yet the theory of permanent revolution — hallmark of 'Trotskyism' — was the object of fierce controversy for years to come. The Mensheviks were naturally appalled by it, but it was too radical for the Bolsheviks as well. Lenin attacked it (without reading it), and only in 1917 did he come to accept the perspective which Trotsky was now offering.

Below: Trotsky with his elder daughter, Zina, photographed in 1906.
Bottom left: The Peter-Paul Fortress, St Petersburg, viewed across the river Neva. Trotsky spent several months there in 1906 while awaiting trial. The prestige of the Soviet was still great, and he had considerable freedom to read and write. His lawyers would carry his manuscripts straight from prison to the printers in their briefcases. 'I feel splendid,' he told visitors. 'I sit and work and feel perfectly sure that I can't be arrested. You will agree that under the conditions in Tsarist Russia, that is rather an unusual sensation.'
Bottom right: Inside the fortress.

Opposite page: Trotsky in his cell. Isaac Deutscher wrote of this photograph: 'The prisoner, lean and of average build, is dressed in black. The black suit, the stiff white collar, the white cuffs slightly protuding from the sleeves and the well-polished shoes give the impression of almost studious elegance. This might have been the picture of a prosperous western European fin-de-siècle intellectual, just about to attend a somewhat formal reception, rather than that of a revolutionary awaiting trial in the Peter-Paul Fortress. Only the austerity of the bare wall and the peephole in the door offer a hint of the real background.'

The trial of the Soviet finally opened on 19 September 1906 before a packed gallery. Things went badly for the prosecution. None of the defendants was in the least penitent, and the police showed themselves to be inept and mendacious. Amid a mounting wave of public sympathy, Trotsky rose to speak on 4 October. His parents were present, at once overawed, terrified and aglow with pride.

'The Prosecution invites us to admit that the Soviet armed the workers for the struggle against the existing "form of government". If I am categorically asked whether this was so, I shall answer: Yes! ... What we have is not a national government but an automaton for mass murder. I can find no other name for the government machine which is tearing into parts the living body of our country. If you tell me that the pogroms, the murders, the burnings, the rapes ... are the form of government of the Russian empire — then I will agree with the prosecution that ... we were arming ourselves, directly and immediately, against the form of government of the Russian Empire.'

On 13 October one of the defending lawyers received a letter from a former director of the police department. This man confirmed that the previous year the police had attempted to organize a pogrom in St Petersburg, but had been thwarted by the Soviet. He continued that General Trepov himself commanded the terrorist 'Black Hundreds', and that the Tsar was regularly

informed of their activities. The defence demanded that the informant, together with the Prime Minister and Minister of the Interior in office at the relevant time, be called to the witness box. The magistrates refused, and the defendants thereafter boycotted the proceedings. On 2 November, in an empty courtroom, Trotsky and others were sentenced to deportation to Siberia for life.

On 5 January 1907 the Soviet prisoners were put aboard a train. Their destination was Obdorsk, a village deep inside the Arctic Circle. Soon they had to travel by sleigh. 'Every day', he wrote to Natalya, 'we descend one degree farther into the kingdom of cold and barbarism.' But on 12 February he escaped, and eleven days later joined Natalya at a railway junction near St Petersburg. He reached Finland before the authorities realized he had gone. He wrote a bestseller entitled 'There and Back', describing his dramatic journey.

Above: Defendants and their lawyers at the trial of the St Petersburg Soviet, 1906. Trotsky is in the centre of the picture, papers in hand. The popularity of the Soviet was immense. 'In the end even the officers of the gendarmerie and the clerks of the court . . . carried flowers from the public to the dock,' he later recalled.

50

Top: Trotsky (second from the left, second row) among his fellow defendants.
Above: Moved before the trial to the House of Preliminary Detention, Trotsky was reunited with Parvus (left) and Leon Deutsch. The latter was an old Narodnik turned Marxist and 'Iskraite' who had befriended Trotsky when the young man first arrived in London. Years later Trotsky recalled in his autobiography: 'There is a photograph showing all three of us in the prison kitchen. The indefatigable Deutsch was planning a wholesale escape for us and easily won Parvus over, insisting that I join them too. I resisted because I was attracted by the political importance of the trial ahead. Too many people were included in the plans, however. In the prison library where they conspired, one of the guards discovered a set of tools. The prison administration hushed the affair up, because the secret police were suspected of planting the tools there to bring about a change in the prison régime. And, after all, Deutsch had to effect his fourth escape not from prison but from Siberia.'

Opposite page: Natalya in Vienna, late 1907. She was pregnant with Sergei (Seryozha). Lyova (or Leon) had been born in 1906, while Trotsky was in prison.

Deportees en route to Obdorsk, January 1907: Trotsky is second from the left. Fourteen prisoners were guarded by 52 soldiers, who could not, however, conceal their sympathy for the Soviet. Secret policemen guarded the guards.

PARIS
LA PRESSE ÉTRANGÈRE

Signature du Titulaire:

Léon Trotsky

In April 1907 Trotsky was back in London, at the Fifth Party Congress — attended by Bolsheviks and Mensheviks. He held himself aloof from both factions. His theory of permanent revolution won the partial support of Rosa Luxemburg, a Polish Marxist who was to lead the revolutionary socialists in Germany until her assassination in 1919. Also present was one Joseph Djugashvili, alias Koba or Stalin, a man closely identified with the Bolsheviks' armed units and on this occasion registered as representing the (bogus) Borchalo branch of the Party. Of the congress Koba reported: 'Somebody among the Bolsheviks remarked jestingly that since the Mensheviks were the faction of the Jews and the Bolsheviks that of native Russians, it would become us to make a pogrom in the Party.'

By the end of 1907 Trotsky and Natalya had moved to Vienna. Their aloofness from the factional struggle commended them to most West European socialists, who considered the Russian split unfortunate at best. Accordingly, Trotsky came to know all the important socialist leaders over the next few years, and saw at first hand how their Marxism was tinged with petty-bourgeois and nationalistic prejudices.

Among the Russians his isolation became ever more complete as he attempted first to reunite Bolsheviks and Mensheviks, and then to unite all and sundry in opposition to Lenin. In 1908 he began publishing a paper called 'Pravda' ('Truth'), but despite a fairly wide circulation in Russia it did not flourish. In 1912 the Bolsheviks killed it off by stealing the name for a rival publication produced in St Petersburg (editor: Stalin).

In 1912 war broke out in the Balkans. The liberal paper 'Kievan Thought' offered him an assignment as war correspondent, and he snatched at the opportunity to escape from émigré circles. Now he saw at first hand where Europe was heading.

Within days of the outbreak of the world war in 1914, the leaders of nearly every socialist party in Europe had dutifully lined up behind their own ruling class. The pretensions of the Second International to unite the workers of the world were at once exposed. Most shocking of all was the self-abasement of the largest workers' party, the German Social Democrats, at the feet of the Kaiser.

Trotsky hurriedly left Vienna for Zurich. With his arrival, a Swiss socialist recalled, 'life returned to the labour movement, or at least to one sector of it. He brought with him the belief ... that from this war would arise revolution.' He dashed off 'The War and the International', the first major anti-war broadside to come from the pen of a Russian:

'We have all gone through the German Socialist school, and learned lessons from its successes as well as its failures. The German Social Democracy was to us not only *a* party of the International. It was *the* party par excellence ... Yet it is just because of this respect for the past, and still more out of respect for the future, which ought to unite the working class of Russia with the working classes of Germany and Austria, that we indignantly reject the "liberating" aid which German imperialism offers us in a Krupp munition box, with the blessing, alas! of German Socialism.'

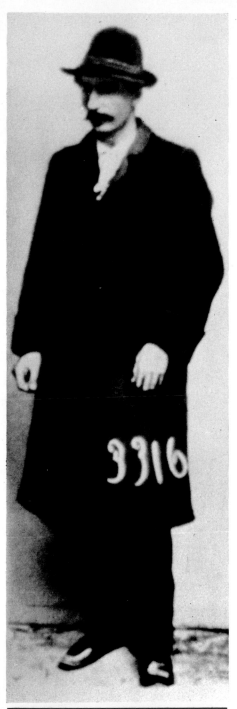

In November he moved to Paris, where he joined Martov in publishing an anti-war paper, 'Golos' ('The Voice'), until the censors shut it in January 1915. But Martov was once again vacillating under pressure from the Menshevik right wing. Trotsky now openly severed his connections with the Mensheviks, broke off relations with former friends such as Parvus who had succumbed to chauvinism, and began to marshal reliable forces around a new paper 'Nashe Slovo' ('Our Word').

On 5 September 1915, thirty-eight delegates representing anti-war parties or factions from eleven countries made their way to the village of Zimmerwald in the Swiss Alps. Trotsky wrote their manifesto:

'Proletarians! Since the outbreak of the war, you have placed your energy, your courage, your endurance at the service of the ruling classes. Now you must stand up for your own cause, for the sacred aims of socialism, for the emancipation of the oppressed nations as well as of the enslaved classes, by means of the irreconcilable proletarian class struggle ... Working men and working women! Mothers and fathers! Widows and orphans! Wounded and crippled! We call to all of you who are suffering from the war and because of the war: beyond all borders, beyond the reeking battlefields, and beyond the devastated cities and villages — Proletarians of all countries unite!'

Sentenced to jail in absentia by a German court for 'The War and the International', Trotsky's position in France also became increasingly precarious. Eventually the Russian Embassy persuaded the French Government to expel him, and he was deported to Spain in September 1916. There he was promptly arrested as a dangerous anarchist. Natalya, Lyova and Seryozha met him in Barcelona just in time to board a boat bound for the United States.

They entered New York harbour on 13 January 1917. Trotsky joined Nikolai Bukharin and Alexandra Kollontai on the editorial board of 'Novy Mir' ('New World'). By the middle of March confused reports were reaching them of disturbances in the Russian capital Petrograd (as St Petersburg was now called). Within days Trotsky was predicting that the Liberals would be swept aside: 'At a meeting of "worthy and most worthy" Russian Social Democrats I read a paper in which I argued that the proletarian party would inevitably assume power in the second stage of the Russian revolution. This produced about the same sort of impression as a stone thrown into a puddle alive with pompous and phlegmatic frogs.'

On 27 March he sailed with his family aboard the Norwegian boat 'Christianafjord', bound for Finland. The ship dropped anchor at Halifax, Nova Scotia, and British naval police dragged them ashore. Trotsky was interned in a concentration camp along with some 800 Germans, mostly sailors. 'The whole month I was there was like one continuous mass meeting. I told the prisoners about the Russian revolution, about Liebknecht (a leading German revolutionary), about Lenin...' German officers and British camp commander were united in their horror at this development, but could do nothing about it. He was freed on 29 April. 'As we were being taken from the camp, our fellow prisoners gave us a most impressive send-off. Although the officers shut themselves up in their compartment, and only a few poked their noses through the chinks, the sailors and workers lined the passage on both sides, an improvised band played the "Internationale", and friendly hands were extended to us from every quarter. One of the prisoners delivered a short speech acclaiming the Russian revolution and cursing the German monarchy.'

They were at sea for nearly three weeks, and then on 17 May (or 4 May, according to the pre-revolutionary calendar) they arrived by train in Petrograd.

Forward

עֶרשֶׁטס

200,000

די בעריהמטע
פון די ערמיסער
אין ריא חוכע דער
ארבייטער וועלבט

VOL. X X   NO. 7123   **NEW YORK, TUESDAY, JANUARY 18.**

גאָלאָסטין קאָם-
באָרדירט.

די בולגאַריסע אַרמיי באַמבאָרדירען   דאָ
שטאַהם אַדיבער דעם הונאַי.—רוסען מאָבען   שטאַרקע אָטאַקעס ביים סערעטה און סר
מטייצע מיד.

בערלין, יאַנ. 15. — דער פֿאָד   שטאַהם וואַרעני, צו דרום-מערב פֿון
נאַרישער קריענס-מיניסטעריום פֿעד   נאָלאָסט, צווישען בוהיי און רעם פֿלאַן
עמענטליכט היינט, אַז די בולגאַריסע   זוא דער סערעטה גאַלם אַריין אין
אַרטילערע באָמבאַרדירם שוין די האַל   דונאַי.

רער אָפֿיציעלער באַריכט פֿון עסטר
(דאָברודשאַ'ר) זיים פֿון דונאַי.

באַזאָרדערם זיינען נעוואָרען די די   וועלדעם:
קאַזאַרבעם און אין כיליסטעריסע נאַבהירעל   צו דרום-מערב
אין נאָלאָסט און דער וואָקזאָל מיט דעם   זואָבען אונזערע באַטאַליאָנען אונטער
אַרטיל-אַרש-בריך לעבען שטעטעל.   רער קאָמאַנדע פֿון נעראַל דעם באַרן 704

די בולנאַריסע ליפֿטמֿליהֿטעֿ האַל   דעם האָללענדישע קריעכם-שיף פֿאָנגם
בען באַמבאַרדירום דעם האַפֿען פֿון סם.   נעמרע אין די לערבֿיאַינע ליפֿטמטמאַל
ציאָן.

די רוסען האָבען שטאַרק אַטאַר   א פֿראָהער יאַנ. 15. — א
קירם לעבען פֿורדעני, אויף דער לינעע ביי   שטשע מעלדעם, אַז א האַלענגריסע טרײַ
רעם אונטערשטען טהײַל פֿון מיד, סער   אַף זיי נעבמען אַקעני מעמ?
רעמה און צווייסען קאַסיא און סוסטעיצא   אַהום האָלענֿר. רי סאָבמאַרין אַיָז אָלעסה
טיכ?ען, לעבען מאָללאווײַער גרעֿנעֿל.   מ?אַלה בעלנינ נעוואָרען אַן מעֿל מֿעַ?
אַבער די.אַלע אטאַקעם הֿינֿעֿ צֿורֿיֿקֿנעֿ?   ק?ֿאַלה בעֿלני?ם ב?ו אֿויֿסֿעֿר רֿיאֿ חֿלֿשֿעֿ
שטֿטֿיֿסֿעֿ נֿעֿוֿאָרֿעֿן.   רֿיֿשֿעֿ וֿאָֿסֿעֿרֿעֿן.

די סֿאֿבֿמֿאֿרֿין אֿויֿז א מֿיֿנֿעֿלֿעֿבֿעֿ
באַרֿ 704 נֿעֿנֿוֿמֿעֿן.   פֿון דֿעֿם זֿעֿברֿוֿכֿעֿנֿעֿר האָֿסֿעֿל. זֿיֿא הֿאָֿסֿ
א פֿרֿעֿהֿעֿרֿטֿיֿנֿעֿר בֿאֿרֿיֿכֿם מֿעֿלֿדֿעֿם,   אֿיֿן א פֿוֿטֿעֿס.
מֿיֿנֿסֿטֿעֿרֿיֿוֿם מֿעֿלֿדֿעֿם, אַז ל?ֿיֿ דֿיֿ רֿיֿימֿעֿר   דֿעֿם 32-קֿאַֿמֿאַֿרֿאֿעֿן. אֿיֿן א פֿוֿטֿעֿס, חֿאָֿבֿ
בֿוֿלֿנֿאַֿרֿיֿסֿע חֿיֿל האֿבֿעֿן נֿעֿנֿוֿמֿעֿן   דֿיֿ אַֿרֿבֿעֿנֿבֿלֿאַֿנֿרֿוֿסֿטֿעֿם פֿוֿן וֿעֿרֿבֿ.

דֿיֿטֿשֿלֿאַֿנֿד   קֿעֿן אֿיֿצֿט נֿיֿם

דאָס איז גענאָסע טראָצקי

רער הֿוֿסֿיֿשֿעֿר-אֿיֿדֿיֿשֿעֿר רֿעֿוֿאָֿלֿו
ציאָנער וֿעֿלֿכֿעֿר אֿיֿז פֿעֿרֿטֿרֿיֿבֿעֿן געֿ
וֿאָֿרֿעֿן פֿוֿן נֿאַֿנֿץ יֿרֿאָֿף, צֿוֿלֿיֿעֿב זֿיֿיֿנֿע
רֿעֿוֿאָֿלֿוֿציֿאָֿנֿעֿרֿעֿ בֿעֿדֿאַֿנֿקֿעֿן.

רֿיֿא בֿיֿלֿד איֿז נֿעֿנֿוֿמֿעֿן געֿוֿאָֿרֿעֿן
נֿעֿכֿטֿעֿן סֿפֿעֿציֿעֿל פֿאַֿר'ן „פֿאָֿרֿוֿוֿעֿרֿדֿסֿ".
אַן אֿויֿסֿסֿיֿרֿיֿעֿרֿלֿיֿבֿעֿן אַֿרֿטֿיֿקֿעֿל וֿיֿעֿגֿעֿן געֿ
טֿרֿאָֿצֿקֿי וֿעֿם רֿעֿר לֿעֿזֿעֿר געֿפֿיֿנֿעֿן אֿויֿף
אַן אֿנֿרֿעֿר פֿיֿרֿדֿיֿם אֿיֿן רֿיֿזֿעֿן נֿוֿמֿעֿר.

אֿיֿעֿר-קֿרֿיֿעֿגֿם א יֿאֿר
פֿרֿיֿאָֿן פֿאַֿר בֿעֿשֿוֿנֿעֿד-
לֿעֿן דֿיֿא גֿעֿרֿעֿכֿטֿיֿגֿקֿיֿם

רֿוֿשֿאֿהֿוֿיֿסֿ שֿהֿאֿבֿאֿאֿ רֿוֿזֿ. חֿיֿיֿם, פֿוֿן
יֿוֿנֿײֿטֿעֿד סֿטֿיֿיֿטֿם רֿיֿסֿטֿרֿיֿקֿם קֿאֿוֿרֿם,
לֿאֿם נֿעֿבֿמֿעֿן מֿעֿרֿ' קֿשֿאַֿמֿם א לֿעֿיֿעֿר צֿו
זֿיֿצֿעֿן א יֿאֿהֿר אֿיֿן פֿרֿיֿזֿאֿן דֿעֿרֿפֿאֿר וֿאֿם
עֿר חֿאֿם 'כֿעֿבֿאֿ'נֿעֿדֿעֿם דֿיֿא גֿעֿרֿעֿכֿטֿיֿן

נֿעֿרֿ-
יֿעֿ-

חֿעֿרֿם פֿעֿר
בֿעֿן רֿעֿגֿוֿעֿ-
לֿאֿוֿסֿאֿ
אֿלֿיֿן מֿעֿנֿעֿרֿ-
אֿיֿז בֿעֿנֿאָֿן

(„נֿאֿסֿעֿ")

אֿאַֿנֿנֿעֿרֿאֿמֿמֿעֿן הֿעֿנֿ-
פֿוֿן אֿיֿעֿר קֿאַֿמֿיֿעֿמֿע.
גֿרֿי אֿיֿז רֿוֿום נֿעֿוֿוֿאָֿ-
וֿואַֿרֿעֿן פֿוֿן נֿאַֿנֿץ יֿרֿאָֿף, צֿוֿלֿיֿעֿב זֿיֿיֿגֿעֿ
חֿאָֿבֿעֿן בֿיֿי אֿיֿהֿם נֿעֿ-
זֿיֿ אֿבֿעֿר קֿאָֿנֿטֿרֿאֿ-
גֿאַֿנֿגֿעֿן מֿיֿט דֿיֿא וֿוֿיֿי-
רֿיֿא שֿמֿיֿמֿע אַֿבֿעֿר אֿוֿן
לֿעֿלֿבֿעֿן עֿר האַֿם נֿעֿ-
חֿאַֿבֿעֿן אֿיֿהֿם פֿעֿרֿ-
אַֿן. אֿנֿרֿעֿר פֿיֿרֿדֿיֿם אֿיֿן רֿיֿזֿעֿן נֿוֿמֿעֿר
נֿעֿוֿוֿעֿן קֿעֿנֿטֿיֿוֿ, אַֿז
רֿיֿפֿעֿנֿרֿעֿנֿם.

מֿראַֿנֿע אֿיֿז נֿעֿוֿוֿעֿן,
זֿיֿעֿן רֿעֿר בֿאַֿנֿקֿיֿעֿר
(„אֿוֿמֿאַֿנֿ'ן) נֿעֿוֿוֿאַֿנֿם
אַֿנֿקֿיֿעֿר, אַֿז עֿר האַֿם נֿעֿ-
א בֿעֿמֿבֿעֿר פֿוֿן קֿאָֿ-
סֿעֿנֿאַֿטֿאָֿר.
אֿיֿז אַֿרֿטֿיֿשֿבֿאַֿלֿדֿ'ר וֿאָֿחֿיֿוֿם,
פֿאַֿרֿיֿם, נֿיֿוֿיֿאָֿרֿק.
מֿעֿרֿעֿ פֿרֿעֿמֿגֿעֿן האַֿם לֿאָֿ'
וֿיֿלֿע, אֿוֿן מֿרֿם וֿוֿיֿסֿקֿאַֿנֿטֿיֿ

Ministère
de l'Intérieur.

Direction
de la
Sûreté Générale.

2e Bureau.

Police des Étrangers.

Expulsion.

République Française.

Le Ministre de l'Intérieur,

Vu l'article 7 de la loi des 13-21 novembre et 3 décembre 1849 ainsi conçu:

"Le Ministre de l'Intérieur pourra par mesure de police, enjoindre à tout étranger voyageant ou résidant en France de sortir immédiatement du territoire français et le faire conduire à la frontière."

Vu l'article 8 de la même loi, ainsi conçu:

"Tout étranger qui se serait soustrait à l'exécution des mesures énoncées dans l'article précédent, ou qui, après être sorti de France par suite de ces mesures y serait rentré sans permission du Gouvernement, sera traduit devant les tribunaux et condamné à un emprisonnement d'un mois à six mois."

"Après l'expiration de sa peine, il sera reconduit à la frontière."

Vu les renseignements recueillis sur le nommé BRONSTEIN-TROTZKY (Léon) sujet russe;

Considérant que la présence de l'étranger sus-désigné sur le territoire français est de nature à compromettre la sûreté publique;

Sur la proposition du Préfet de police

Arrête :

Article 1er.

Il est enjoint au nommé BRONSTEIN-TROTZKY (Léon) de sortir du territoire français.

Article 2.

Le Préfet de Police est chargé de l'exécution du présent arrêté.

A Paris, le 14 SEPT 1916

Signé: MALVY.

Pour ampliation:

Pour le Directeur de la Sûreté Générale:

Le Chef du 2e Bureau.

Above: The offices of 'Novy Mir', 177 St Mark's Place, Lower East Side, New York.
Left: The order expelling Trotsky from France, 16 September 1916.
Below: Internment papers issued by the British Government. No written grounds for his arrest were produced.
Opposite page: Trotsky reunited with his younger daughter Nina in Petrograd, 1917, after eleven years' separation.

PRISONERS OF WAR.

[Form to be completed in respect of each Prisoner of War immediately on his arrival at his first place of Internment. When completed it should be transmitted in original to the "Prisoners of War Information Bureau," 49, Wellington Street, Strand, London, W.C., England. The entries on the back of the form (Part II) should be completed by the Prisoner of War himself.]

PART I.

(Portion of the Form to be filled up by the O.C. Place of Internment.)

Place of Internment ___Amherst. N.S___

Date ___April 3/17___

GENERAL No.	SURNAME OF PRISONER	CHRISTIAN NAMES IN FULL
1098. [This is the serial No. given to the Prisoner in the Register of the Place of Internment.]	Trotsky	Leon, Bronstein

Place of Capture ___Halifax. N.S.___

Date of Capture ___3-4-17___

Date of Internment ___3-4-17___

From whom received ___Capt McClave F.I.O. Halifax. N.S.___

HEIGHT ft. in.	WEIGHT lbs.	COMPLEXION	HAIR	EYES	MARKS (if any)
5-8½	190	Dark, Moustache, Beard noted	Black	Black	Thumb prints

Nature of wounds (if any):

Special observations:

Personal effects (if any) to be enumerated: Left. Right.

For use of P.W.I.B.
Entered
Checked

M.F.W. 1

Signature _____ Col.

O.C. Internment Station, Amherst.

[TURN OVER]

PART II.

Portion of the form to be filled up by the Prisoner himself, if possible, otherwise at his dictation.

Dieser Teil des Formulars ist wo möglich von dem Kriegsgefangenen selbst auszufüllen. Im Falle seiner Unfähigkeit soll das Ausfüllen nach seinem Diktat erfolgen.

Bitte recht deutlich schreiben.
Please write distinctly.

	Familienname / Surname	Vornamen. (Bloße Initialbuchstaben sind nicht genügend) / Christian name (in full)	Alter / Age
1.	Trotsky	Leon, Bronstein	39 y'd

		Regiment, (bezw. Bataillon) oder sonstige Abteilung. Schiff, (bezw. Boot) oder Division / Unit	Regiments-nummer / No. of the Unit	Legitimations-nummer / Identification No.
2.	Dienstgrad (Rangstufe) / Rank			

3. Gehören Sie zum Aktiv, zur Reserve, zur Ersatzreserve, zur Landwehr, Seewehr, oder zum Landsturm? State whether with the Colours or in the Reserve. — Political Exile. Have not escaped Military Service.

4. Beruf: / Occupation: Journalist

5. Geburtsort / Place of Birth — Es wird nach möglichst genauen Angaben verlangt / Full particulars are required

Ortschaft / City, Township, Village	Staat / Kingdom, Duchy, etc.	Provinz, Regierungsbezirk oder Kreis / Administrative Divisions
Janowka	Chersou	Russia

6. Staatsangehörigkeit: / Nationality: Russian

7. Privatadresse: / Home address: Wife taken off Halifax. N.S. from same ship.

8. Unterschrift des Kriegsgefangenen: / Prisoner of War's signature: Russian Citizen Leon Trotsky

9. Datum: / Date: 3/4/17

On arrival at the Finland station,
Petrograd, 4 May 1917,
Trotsky exhorts the crowd to prepare
for a workers' revolution.

Russian troops greet the revolution, 1917.

REVOLUTION RUSSIA 1917-1921

Lenin and Trotsky symbolized the victorious workers' revolution. Many Russian peasants believed they were one and the same person.

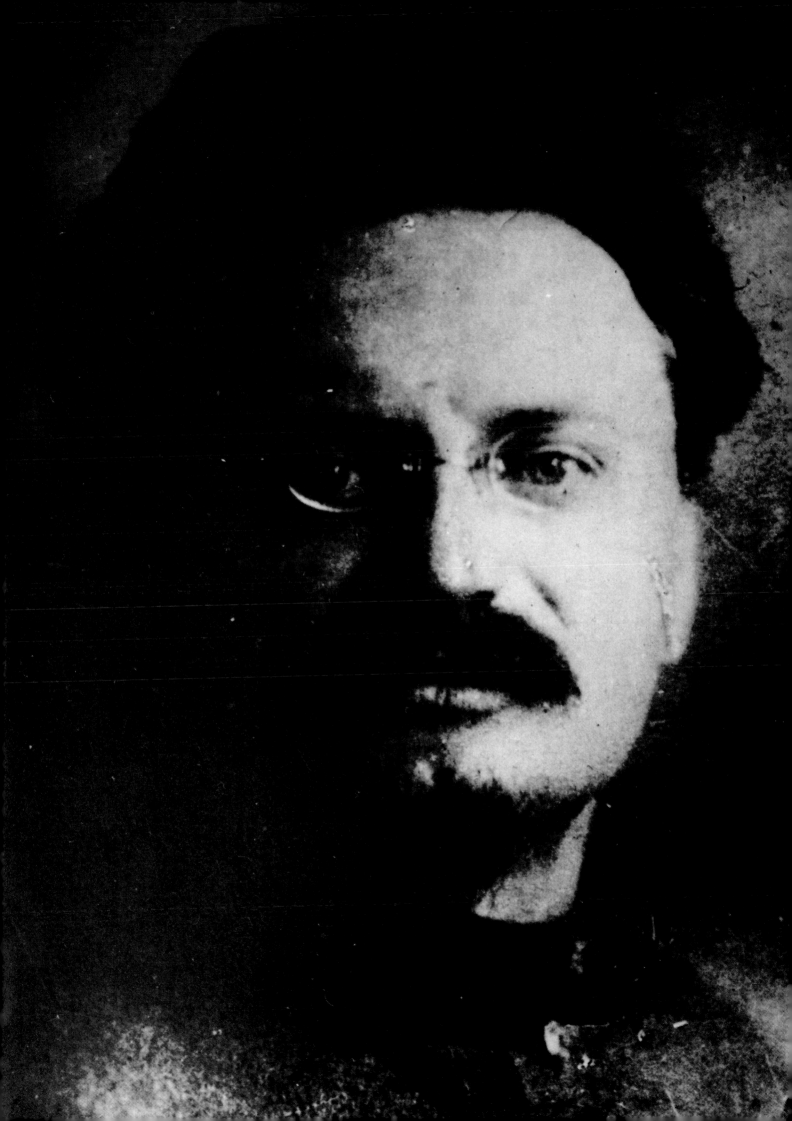

The war had brought devastation to Russia. By the beginning of 1917 inflation was rampant, there were fuel and food shortages in the cities, and above all the workers and peasants hated the war and the imperial government that waged it.

On 23 February, International Women's Day, women textile workers went on strike in Petrograd and called the metalworkers out with them. By the 25th a quarter of a million workers were demonstrating against the government. Troops sent to restore order defected to the revolution.

The Petrograd Soviet of Workers' and Soldiers' Deputies sprang into being on the 27th. It was dominated by Mensheviks and Socialist Revolutionaries (populists, heirs to the Narodnik tradition; known as the SRs). They occupied one wing — appropriately, the left — of the Tauride Palace, while at the other end of the corridor the liberals appointed themselves a Provisional Government. Two powers stood side by side.

At first the Soviet parties supported the government without joining it. But the

liberals' pro-war policies led to the collapse of their Cabinet. To save the government Menshevik and SR delegates formed a coalition with the liberals under Alexander Kerensky on 5 May. On the same day Trotsky made his first speech to the Soviet. He was coolly received by the majority, but was elected to the Executive Committee on a proposal from the Bolsheviks.

The Bolshevik Party grew rapidly. Its membership in Petrograd rose between February and April from 2,000 to 16,000, though elsewhere its influence was less dominant. Trotsky became the capital's most popular orator; even Lenin's light, many felt, shone dimly in comparison.

Above: Delegates to the Petrograd Soviet of Workers' and Soldiers' Deputies, 1917. Trotsky is seated seventh from the left, second row from the front. The Soviet was composed mostly of factory delegates.

At the beginning of July the revolutionary mood burst forth in an armed demonstration which the Bolsheviks had been unable to prevent. The Provisional Government seized the opportunity to suppress the party's Petrograd headquarters and arrest its leading members. Lenin and his second-in-command, Grigori Zinoviev, went into hiding. Trotsky remained free until the 23rd, defending the Bolsheviks as best he could before he himself was arrested, charged with treason and thrown into Kresty prison.

In those days, according to Fyodor Raskolnikov, a Bolshevik leader at the Kronstadt naval base, 'at every crossroads all you could hear was curses on the Bolsheviks. It was dangerous to show oneself openly in the street as a member of our party.' This mood encouraged the reactionaries to seek a permanent end to the red menace. General Kornilov planned a military conquest of the capital. At first Kerensky connived with him, but then took fright.

At the end of August Kornilov declared war on the Kerensky régime and ordered his army, headed by the infamous Savage Division, to begin the offensive. The government collapsed, the rich fled the city, and Kerensky found himself bereft of all support. Workers, sailors, soldiers — all backed the Bolsheviks. Trotsky remembered: 'The sailors from the "Aurora" sent a special delegation to the prison to ask my advice: should they defend the Winter Palace (now the seat of the Provisional Government) or take it by assault? I advised them to put off the squaring of their account with Kerensky until they had finished Kornilov. "What's ours will not escape us." '

Bolshevik agitators corroded Kornilov's army while Bolshevik Red Guards, armed by Bolshevik troops, defended the city's suburbs. The counter-revolution collapsed without a serious fight.

Trotsky was freed on 4 September. Kerensky, liberals, Mensheviks and SRs were now all in utter disarray. The Bolsheviks won a majority in the Petrograd Soviet under the slogan 'All power to the Soviets'. Moscow and other centres soon followed. On the 23rd the Petrograd Soviet elected Trotsky as its President. He mounted the dais to 'a hurricane of

70

applause', according to the contemporary historian Sukhanov. 'This was now once again a revolutionary army ... This was Trotsky's guard, ready at a wink from him to storm the coalition, the Winter Palace and all the fortresses of the bourgeoisie.'

Preparations were now underway for the insurrection which was to bring the working class to power for the first time in history. On 9 October the Soviet formed the Military Revolutionary Committee, command centre of the revolution. The date was set: 25 October, the day the second all-Russia Congress of Soviets was due to meet. One after another army and naval units declared for revolution. Trotsky's headquarters were in the Smolny Institute:

'On the night of the 24th the members of the Revolutionary Committee went out into the various districts, and I was left alone. Later on Kamenev came in. He was opposed to the uprising, but he had come to spend that night with me, and together we stayed in the tiny corner room on the third floor, so like the captain's bridge on that deciding night of the revolution.'

By daybreak the following morning the strategic points of the city were under Bolshevik control, with the exception of the Winter Palace, where officer cadets and the Women's Battalion of Death held out. The Congress of Soviets opened to the roar of the 'Aurora's' guns — firing blanks at the Palace, which promptly surrendered. The Bolsheviks had an absolute majority of delegates. They gave Lenin an immense accolade as he announced: 'We will now proceed to build the socialist order.'

The two leaders of the revolution find a quiet moment together. 'Lenin has not yet had time to change his collar, but his eyes are very wide awake, even though his face looks so tired. He looks softly at me, with that sort of awkward shyness that with him indicates intimacy. "You know," he says hesitatingly, "from persecution and a life underground, to come so suddenly into power ... it makes you giddy," and he circles his hand around his head. We look at each other and laugh a little. All this takes only a moment or two; then we "pass on to next business". '

Top right: A meeting of Soviet Commissars soon after the October Revolution. Trotsky is seated second from the left, Zinoviev second from the right. Fyodor Raskolnikov is standing in the centre of the picture (marked 6).
Right: Fourteen thousand Kronstadt sailors march to the defence of Petrograd against General Kornilov's counter-revolutionary army, August 1917.
Left: Alexander Kerensky. In the early days of the revolution, when the Russian workers and peasants were awakening politically, his histrionic speeches were greeted with rapture. But the polarization of political attitudes left him without supporters. After the October Revolution he attempted to march on Petrograd at the head of a Cossack army, but had to flee in disguise to avoid being arrested by his own troops. He passed his later life in the USA.

Red Guard Unit outside the Nikolayevsky station in Moscow, 1917. These worker volunteers were the shock troops of the revolution.

Захватъ власти большевиками въ Петроградъ.

Фотографіи для «Огонька».

1) Тов Ленинъ (г. Ульяновъ), предсѣдатель совѣта народныхъ комиссаровъ. (Мы вынуждены помѣстить старый портретъ Ленина, такъ какъ, по его заявленію, онъ снимется только тогда, когда у него отрастутъ усы и борода, сбритые для лучшаго замаскированія, послѣ отдачи приказа Временнаго Правительства объ его арестѣ). 2) Тов. Троцкій (г. Бронштейнъ), комиссаръ по иностраннымъ дѣламъ и предсѣдатель петроградскаго С. Р. и С. Д. 3) Г. Луначарскій, комиссаръ по народному образованію. 4) Тов. Абрамъ (г. прапорщикъ Крыленко), комиссаръ по военнымъ дѣламъ и верховный главнокомандующій россійскими арміями и флотомъ. 5) Тов. Каменевъ (г. Розенфельдъ), одинъ изъ энергичнѣйшихъ дѣятелей большевистскаго переворота. 6) Матросъ Дыбенко, комиссаръ по морскимъ дѣламъ. 7) Тов. Антоновъ (г. Овсѣенко), главнокомандующій войсками петроградскаго военнаго округа 8) Г-жа Коллонтай, комиссаръ по общественному призрѣнію. 9) Засѣданіе революціоннаго комитета.

Above: Contemporary photomontage of the Bolshevik leaders of the revolution. It will be noticed that Joseph Stalin was not among them.

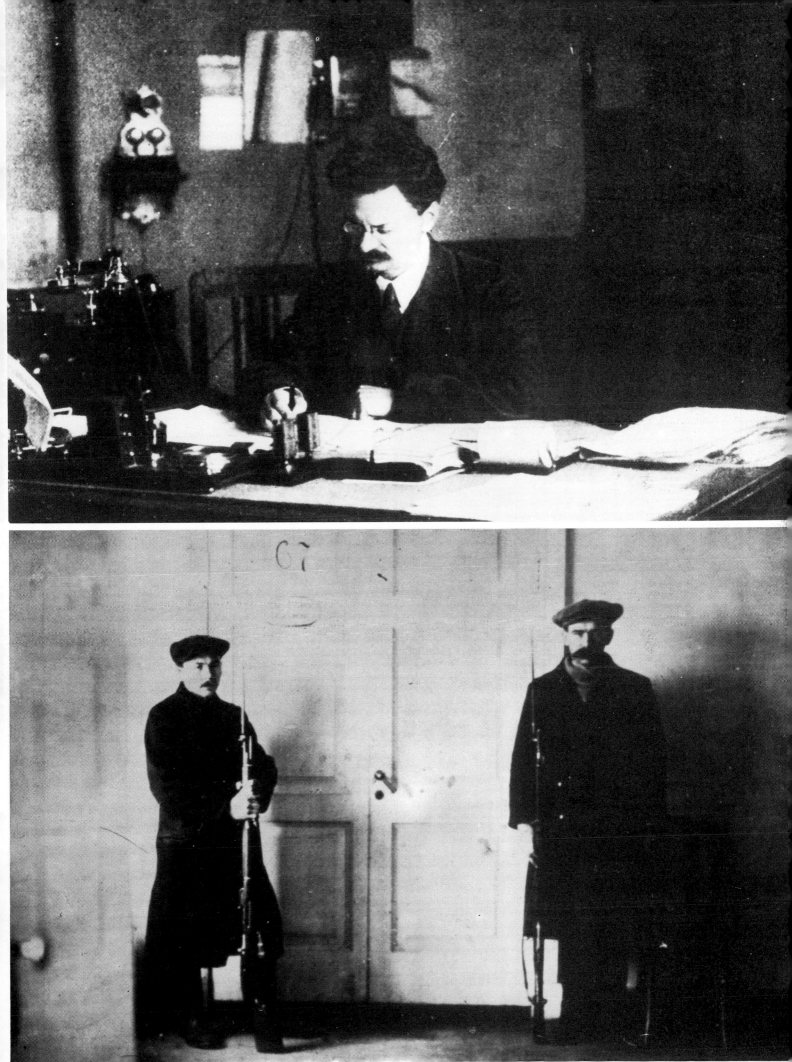

Top: Trotsky at work in the Smolny Institute, where the Bolshevik revolution was organized. Above: Red Guard sentries outside his office.

The Bolsheviks had not marched in perfect formation towards the revolution. At first the leadership in Russia pursued policies hardly different from those of the Mensheviks and SRs: support for the Provisional Government as long as it acted progressively. The revolution was to be bourgeois in character, with socialism as an 'ultimate goal'.

Lenin had tried to change the party's course from abroad with a series of articles known as 'Letters from Afar'. Stalin edited them to remove the 'rough edges'. Stalin was for fusion with the Mensheviks. Immediately on his arrival in Petrograd on 3 April, Lenin demanded that the party prepare itself to lead a socialist revolution. The following day he drew up his 'April Theses' — and could not find a single party leader to sign them with him. Instead he was denounced for 'Trotskyism'. But the worker membership of the party stood to the left of its leaders, and before the end of the month Lenin had won the Bolsheviks to revolution.

When Trotsky returned to Petrograd he joined a small group, the Mezhrayontsi ('Inter-Borough Organization'), which had grown up in the capital during the war under the influence of his writings. Nothing save the label now separated this group from the Bolsheviks. It remained only for Trotsky to acknowledge that he had been wrong in his attacks on Lenin's party-building strategy. This he did, and led his followers into the Bolshevik Party. Some 4,000 joined Lenin's party on 26 July. Trotsky received 131 delegates' votes (out of 134) in the election to the fused Central Committee, Lenin 133.

At the end of September Lenin was again struggling with his Central Committee, insisting that preparations begin at once for the seizure of power. His articles for 'Pravda' were again censored by Stalin. But on 10 October he finally committed the party to an uprising. Zinoviev and Kamenev voted against. They then denounced the decision in a newspaper produced by the writer Maxim Gorky, an action Lenin described as 'treacherous and strike-breaking'.

After the seizure of power another vicious row erupted. The left wing of the SRs, some of whom had supported the insurrection, were demanding that a coalition government be formed, and that Lenin and Trotsky be excluded from it. The majority of the Bolshevik Central Committee rejected these demands, but Zinoviev, Kamenev and three others resigned. A split in the ruling party seemed quite probable, but the Left SRs withdrew their demands and presently accepted the minority of government posts offered by the Bolsheviks. Zinoviev and Kamenev returned to the fold once more.

The most urgent task facing the new government was to end Russia's involvement in the war. Trotsky became People's Commissar for Foreign Affairs. He negotiated an armistice with the Germans, and on 27 December travelled to Brest Litovsk for peace talks.

The Germans were anxious to transfer troops from the Eastern to the Western Front before the British and French won a major victory. More importantly, the Bolsheviks knew that revolution would soon break out in Germany — and this, they believed, was the key to their own survival. So Trotsky played for time. He used the negotiations to appeal directly to the working class of the belligerent nations to abandon the war and turn their guns on their own rulers.

But soon an answer had to be made to the Germans' demands. These were draconian: among other things, they wanted Poland, Lithuania, Estonia, Finland and the Ukraine. Quite apart from the territorial and economic damage such concessions would cause, the lives of revolutionaries in these countries would be put at risk.

One faction of the Bolsheviks, led by Bukharin and Karl Radek, was for a 'revolutionary war' to drive out the Germans and carry the revolution abroad by force of arms. The Left SRs also supported this position. But the Russian trenches were empty and

Above: Left to right, M. N. Pokrovsky, Admiral Altvater, Adolf Yoffe and Trotsky on their way to the Brest Litovsk peace conference, December 1917.
Opposite page: 'From October to Brest Litovsk', and heavily corrected pages of Trotsky's original manuscript.

the army dispersed; Lenin, on the contrary, wanted to sign a peace treaty immediately at all costs. He argued that the revolution must buy time.

Trotsky took an intermediate position, which he summed up as 'neither peace nor war'. He was not sure that the Germans were capable of mounting a serious offensive, and would not agree to sign a peace treaty until a major attack was underway.

As if in vindication of his position, strikes broke out in Vienna, Berlin and other cities in early January 1918. Soviets were proclaimed. Much to the amazement of the Austro-Germans, Trotsky announced on the 28th: 'We are demobilizing our army. We refuse to sign a peace based on annexations. We declare that the state of war between the Central Empires and Russia is at an end.'

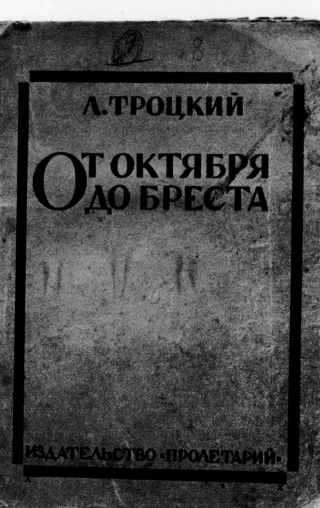

The German revolution did not triumph in spring 1918, as the Bolsheviks so ardently hoped. The workers' movement was rapidly suppressed, and on 18 February the German army under General Hoffman — 'that gangster in a helmet', as Trotsky had described him — resumed the offensive. They met no resistance, and Petrograd was soon **80** threatened.

Trotsky now sided with Lenin, and it was agreed to sue for peace. A peace treaty was signed on 3 March. But the complexity — and apparent inconsistency — of Trotsky's behaviour had earned him few admirers.

The Left SRs denounced the peace as a betrayal. Their members resigned all their positions in the Council of People's Commissars (the chief institution of the revolutionary government), though they did not entirely withdraw from government activity or

from the Cheka (the political police). But this half-in, half-out policy clearly could not be sustained for long.

On 6 July, as the Fifth Congress of Soviets met in Moscow, two Left SRs assassinated Count Mirbach, the German Ambassador. This was the signal for a general uprising, but in the event it failed miserably — more, it seems, from lack of conviction on the part of the SRs themselves than from military measures taken against them by the

Bolsheviks. Within two days their insurrection had collapsed. Almost the entire Left SR leadership was arrested.

The SRs, once the greatest political force in Russia, were now ground to dust between the Bolsheviks and the counter-revolution. Many denounced their leaders and joined the Bolsheviks, while others reverted to acts of individual terrorism against them. On 31 August a Moscow SR, Fanny Kaplan, fired three shots point-blank at Lenin as he was leaving a factory meeting, hitting him in the neck and shoulder. He nearly died of his wounds. While he lay unconscious the Bolsheviks' enemies felt the first hot breath of the Red Terror.

State power thus became concentrated exclusively in the Bolsheviks' hands. They had not sought this monopoly, nor did they shrink from it.

Above: Lenin presiding over a meeting of the Soviet of People's Commissars in the Kremlin, 17 October 1918. This was his first public appearance since Kaplan's assassination attempt six weeks earlier. Trotsky (who also escaped assassination in August) is seated beneath the map.

During the revolution the old Tsarist army had completely disintegrated. The peasant conscripts had returned home to share in the distribution of land from the large estates. As a rule, the most revolutionary regiments were most affected.

At the beginning of 1918 there were some 25,000 Red Guards in Petrograd and smaller numbers elsewhere. These were workers recruited in the factories. They showed great heroism and class-consciousness, but lacked military training and organization. Small guerrilla bands also sprang into being in the countryside to defend the land which the revolution had given them. They were often very active, especially in Siberia, but they were no match for regular forces.

'History', Lenin once said, 'causes the military problem to become the essence of the political problem.' Trotsky was called upon to solve the problem when, in March 1918, he was appointed Commissar of War and President of the Supreme War Council. Within two and a half years he had created a Red Army of five million. Beginning with the core of Communists in the Red Guards, he continually expanded his armies first with volunteers (by May 1918 the Red Volunteer Army was 306,000 strong), then by absorbing the guerrillas and through conscription.

This force defeated several major White (counter-revolutionary) offensives backed by armies of intervention from fifteen countries: Germany, Britain, France, the United States,

Japan, Czechoslovakia, Greece, Poland, Latvia, Finland, Estonia, Yugoslavia, Rumania, Lithuania and Turkey. Fortunately for the young Soviet state, these countries and their counter-revolutionary allies failed to achieve much coordination. They also operated from the extremes of the Soviet Union, whereas the Reds defended an inner circle and could more easily concentrate their forces.

The Civil War was fought over vast distances: in 1919 the 5th Red Army under Tukhachevsky mounted an attack which covered 8,000 kilometres, from the Volga to Vladivostok. Under these conditions the railways assumed great strategic importance. Trotsky equipped a train as his mobile headquarters. It was armour-plated and carried heavy guns and a force of crack troops which would be thrown into battle wherever the defensive line threatened to give way. It was also an administrative centre, as Trotsky remembered: 'Its sections included a secretariat, a printing-press, a telegraph station, a radio station, an electric-power station, a library, a garage and a bath. The train was so heavy that it needed two engines.' He lived on that train, except for brief interludes, for two and a half years.

Above: Parade marking the first anniversary of the revolution, Red Square, November 1918.

Trotsky and the train of the Predrevoyensoviet —
President of the Revolutionary War Council —
visiting the Western front. In 1919 the train as a whole
was decorated with the Order of the
Red Flag for its role in the defence of Petrograd.

The Civil War began in earnest in May 1918. A Czechoslovak Legion, 40,000 strong, revolted at the instigation of the British and French. Meeting negligible resistance, they seized 3,000 kilometres of the Trans-Siberian Railway. This was the signal for a rising of Cossacks in the south. The Germans were pressing in from the west while Whites under the protection of Britain were moving towards Petrograd from Archangel.

By mid-summer Moscow itself (now the country's capital) was threatened. Trotsky moved his train up to the front line at Svyazhsk, declaring that he would not yield an inch of territory. The revolutionaries, heavily outnumbered, were taken from behind in a surprise attack by a large force of White Guards. 'Trotsky mobilized the whole personnel of the train — the clerks, telegraphists, ambulancemen and his own bodyguard — in short, every man who could hold a rifle,' recalled Larissa Reissner, a

writer and Red Army volunteer who was present. 'The White Guards thought they were fighting a new, well-organized body of troops that their intelligence services did not know about; they did not guess that all the opposition they had to encounter was a hastily assembled handful of fighters, behind whom there was nobody but Trotsky himself and Slavin, the commander of the 5th Red Army.' The Whites were routed. The following day Trotsky had twenty-seven deserters, including Communists, shot. But morale was restored, and the Red Army swept forward to dramatic victories at Simbirsk and Kazan.

Above: Trotsky on the Volga during the Civil War. He dressed the crew of his train in leather uniforms, 'which always makes men look heavily imposing'.

Red soldiers on one of the armoured trains which played such a decisive role in the Civil War. These men are evidently about to bury a comrade: his coffin rests on top of the train. He may have been killed by the shell which pierced the turret.

The President of the Revolutionary War Council reviews troops at the front before battle.

Matters went less well on the southern front, commanded at Tsaritsyn by a former NCO, Klim Voroshilov, who refused to take orders from the central command. This 'NCO Clique' formed the backbone of the Military Opposition to Trotsky. They opposed conscription, favoured guerrilla against regular war; demanded the election rather than appointment of officers; and above all objected to the employment of former Tsarist officers. Voroshilov's group was cultivated by Stalin, who became such a menace that Trotsky

who became such a menace that Trotsky

had to have him removed to Moscow.

The Voroshilov clique was especially enraged at the appointment of Mikhail Tukhachevsky to command the First Red Army, of which their force supposedly formed a part. Tukhachevsky, a former Lieutenant of the Guards who had come over to the Bolsheviks, proclaimed the mobilization of all former Tsarist officers. Voroshilov responded by threatening to shoot the 'Guards Officer' if he dared to set foot in Tsaritsyn. The combined authority of Lenin and Trotsky was required to suppress these indications of open rebellion, but Voroshilov

still made trouble for the Red Army command. He excused his own inactivity in the field by claiming that he was being starved of arms. A good part of Trotsky's time was consumed in refuting these charges.

At first Lenin, too, expressed reservations about the use of former Tsarist officers in the Red Army, and wondered whether they could not be phased out. Trotsky informed him there were 30,000 such officers in the Red Army. Each officer was shadowed by a political commissar and, as Trotsky delicately explained: 'commissars were required to keep a record of the families of officers and

admit them to posts of authority provided it were possible in the event of a betrayal of faith to detain the family in question'. Lenin, who was at the time trying to press former factory managers into the service of Soviet industry, appreciated the force of Trotsky's arguments. He said of this conversation: 'I gained a concrete conception of what constitutes the secret of making proper use of our enemy ... of how to build communism out of the bricks that the capitalists had gathered to use against us.'

Above left: Trotsky in conversation with General Sergei Kamenev, a former Tsarist commander whom Trotsky recruited to the service of the revolution.
Above: Key figures in the 'NCO Clique' — Voroshilov (top) and Stalin at Tsaritsyn in the summer of 1918.
Left: Admiral Kolchak, White commander in the east, recognized by the signatories to the Treaty of Versailles as Russian head of state. He shot himself in 1920.

Austro-German troops executing revolutionary workers in Ekaterinoslav (now Dnepropetrovsk) in the Ukraine, 1918. This region suffered some of the bloodiest outrages in a notoriously cruel civil war. Western socialists visiting Moscow commented on the change that had been wrought in Trotsky; Arthur Ransome wrote that he was 'a strange figure for those who had known him as one of the greatest anti-militarists in Europe'. In truth he had never been a pacifist, but the transition from Western intellectual to Red Army commander must have been traumatic nevertheless. The writer Isaac Babel, another Jew 'with spectacles on his nose', struggled to come to terms with the savagery of the Civil War in a series of stories entitled 'Red Cavalry'. They reflect his experiences as a volunteer in a revolutionary Cossack regiment, and were highly regarded by Trotsky (though not by Babel's commander, Budienny). This is an extract from 'A Letter':

'Dear Mother, Evdokia Fyodorovna, In the first lines of this letter I hasten to let you know that, thanks to the Lord, I am alive and well which I would like to hear the same from you . . . In the second lines of this letter I hasten to describe to you about Dad, that he killed my brother Theodore a year ago. Our Red brigade was advancing under Comrade Pavlichenko on the town of Rostov when treason took place in our tanks. Dad was then with General Denikin, commanding a company. Them as saw him said he wore medals on him like under the old régime. And they took us all prisoners because of that treason and my brother Theodore came to Dad's notice. And Dad began cutting him about, saying, "Brute, Red cur, son of a bitch," and all sorts of other things, and went on cutting him about until it grew dark and Theodore passed away ... I soon ran away from Dad and managed to get to my unit under Comrade Pavlichenko ... Then we began to pursue General Denikin, and killed thousands of them, and drove them into the Black Sea. Only Dad was nowhere to be seen and brother Simon looked everywhere for him because he missed brother Theo very much. Only, Dear Mother, you know Dad and his pig-headed character, so what d'you think he did? He dyed his beard shamelessly from red to black and was staying in the town of Maykop in civvies so that none of the inhabitants knew that he was the same as was a cop under the old régime. But the truth will out ... Simon gave the dirty Yids a rough time of it for not handing Dad over but putting him under lock and key in prison, saying as an order had come from Comrade Trotsky not to kill prisoners and saying we'll judge him ourselves, don't you worry, he'll get what he deserves ... But Simon got Dad all right and he began to whip Dad and lined up all the fighting men in the yard according to army custom. Then Simon dashed water over Dad's beard, and asked him:

"You all right, Dad, in my hands?"

"No," says Dad, "not all right."

Then Simon said: "And Theo, was he all right in your hands when you killed him?"

"No," says Dad. "Things went badly for Theo."

Then Simon asked: "And did you think, Dad, that things would go badly for you?"

"No," says Dad, "I didn't think things would go badly for me."

Then Simon turned to us all and said: "And what I think is that if I got caught by his boys, there wouldn't be no quarter for me. — And now, Dad, we're going to finish you off ... " '

Above: A section of one of the Red Army's armoured trains. The trains were not only fighting units: some, such as the propaganda train 'October Revolution', were equipped with mobile cinemas, film crews and printing presses, and Trotsky went out of his way to recruit poets and artists to his own train.

Left: Trotsky and his personal staff. We know some of their names: Butov, Glazman, Syermuks, Poznansky and Nechayev were all executed or driven to suicide by the Stalin regime in later years.

Right: General Anton Denikin, commander of White forces in the south in 1919. The British government gave him £14,500,000, but money could not buy a reliable army.

In the spring of 1919 General Denikin assumed control of White forces in the south, and advanced rapidly through the Caucasus and Ukraine. By early autumn he was threatening Moscow, but his very success sowed the seeds of his downfall. His army had originally been composed of volunteers, whose dedication to counter-revolution was sure. But now he resorted to conscription, and his forces began to crumble from within. In September he suffered a serious defeat at the hands of Nestor Makhno's 'Ukrainian Army of Insurgent Peasants', which flew the black flag of anarchy. The following month the Reds recaptured Orel, and Denikin's army broke into full flight. He managed to evacuate only a few remnants by sea to the Crimea.

Meanwhile a 'Government of the North-West' had been formed with the assistance of the British, who had occupied Archangel. General Yudenich assembled an army 70,000 strong and swept south towards Petrograd. The threat was so serious that Lenin wanted to abandon the city. Trotsky categorically refused to allow it, and rushed to the spot. He mobilized the entire population to dig defences around the city. Then on 18 October he succeeded in halting the Red Army's retreat by — literally — chasing the troops forward on horseback. Within weeks the Whites were defeated, and the British were forced to evacuate Archangel. They left Yudenich behind to meet his fate.

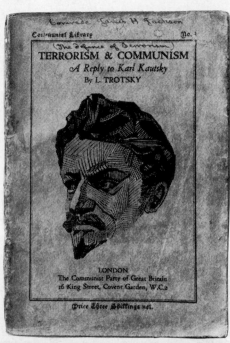

Top left: Trotsky's anti-war pamphlet 'War and Revolution', originally published in German in 1914, was reproduced in this abbreviated edition by the Socialist Labour Party in Glasgow in 1918.
Top centre: Two articles on 'The Economy in Soviet Russia and West Europe: Collapse and Reconstruction', by Rykov (then head of the Supreme Economic Council) and Trotsky, published in Berlin in 1920.
Top right: Karl Kautsky, founder of the

German Social Democratic Party, was for many years held in great esteem by Lenin and Trotsky. But in 1918 he denounced the Bolshevik revolution, accusing them of abandoning Marxism for terrorism. Trotsky replied with a devastating polemic.
Above: 'The highest authority in the Russian Soviet Republic: The Soviet of People's Commissars'. Mikhail Kalinin, President of the Republic, is flanked by Lenin and Trotsky.

Opposite page: A contemporary montage showing Comrade Trotsky, tirelessly active on the various Civil War fronts.

Товарищ Троцкий

The last major offensive mounted with direct imperialist support began in the summer of 1920, when a force under Baron Wrangel advanced from the Crimea. With the assistance of the French he had rallied the forces dispersed during the rout of Denikin. In September he attacked the industrial area of the Don Basin. Trotsky set off in his train for the Crimea to prepare a counter-offensive. He wrote in his train newspaper, 'En Route': 'Our train is again bound for the front ... There now is left only the Crimea, which the French government has made its fortress. The White Guard garrison of this French fortress is under the command of a hired German-Russian general, Baron Wrangel. The friendly family of our train is starting on a new campaign. Let this campaign be the last.' Before October was out, five of Wrangel's divisions had been annihilated in a single day by the Red Cavalry.

By mid-November Sevastopol was in Soviet hands, and after a savage battle on the Perekop Isthmus Wrangel's army was driven into the sea.

Once the threat from the Whites had been eliminated, the shaky alliance formed between the Red Army and Nestor Makhno's Blacks came to an end. Makhno had assembled a force of some 15,000, but they were no match for the Red Cavalry, commanded by Semyon Budienny, himself a former guerrilla commander. Makhno fought on desperately until August 1921, finally reaching the Rumanian frontier with a handful of men. From there he fled to France.

Opposite page, top: Red sailors in Petrograd, leaving for battle against Yudenich, 1919.

Opposite page, centre: Trotsky in conference with Bela Kun (Hungarian revolutionary leader), Alfred Rosmer (French revolutionary and personal friend of Trotsky's from before the war), M.V. Frunze (who commanded the last offensive against Wrangel in 1920) and S.I. Gusev.

Above: Nestor Makhno, charismatic leader of the Ukrainian anarchists, with some of his troops. In October 1920 Kun, Frunze and Gusev signed a treaty of alliance with him on behalf of the Red Army, but it was soon scrapped. After his defeat Makhno fled to Paris, where he died in 1934, an alcoholic factory worker.

Far left: A detachment of the First Red Cavalry.

Left: Baron Petr Wrangel, commander of the last counter-revolutionary offensive, 1920.

Lenin and Trotsky at a demonstration
marking the second anniversary of the revolution,
7 November 1919.

Ever since the collapse of the Second International into craven nationalism at the outbreak of the World War in 1914, the Bolsheviks had aimed to create a new international. The conference at Zimmerwald in 1915 was a step towards that goal. The Russian revolution itself, and the ending of the war, swung working-class politics sharply to the left throughout the world. In many countries new parties, or fractions of the old

socialist parties, emerged with a political outlook similar to that of the Russian Communist Party (as the Bolsheviks had renamed their organization).

At the beginning of 1919 Lenin called upon the left internationally to send delegates to Moscow. Despite the war of intervention and a total imperialist blockade of the Soviet state, fifty-one delegates from thirty-three organizations assembled on 2 March for the founding conference of the Third International.

Trotsky arrived straight from the Kolchak front, and made a dramatic impression. 'If you draw a straight line on the map, radiating from Moscow in any direction,' he told the delegates, 'you will find everywhere at the front a Russian peasant, a Russian worker standing in this cold night, gun in hand, at the frontiers of the Socialist Republic and defending it. And I can assure you that the worker-Communists who comprise the hard core of this army feel that they are not only the Guards Regiment of the Russian

Socialist Republic but also the Red Army of the Third International.' He also wrote the manifesto of the new international.

In fact, the prospects for successful revolution outside Russia, which had seemed so bright the year before, had just suffered a serious setback: in January the German Spartacus League was provoked into an ill-organized and poorly supported uprising in Berlin. It was quickly suppressed with the assistance of the Social Democrats, and on the 15th Karl Liebknecht and Rosa Lux-

emburg were murdered. The German Communist movement never fully recovered from the blow, despite further revolutionary upheavals. Within a month of the conference, Soviet states were proclaimed in Bavaria and Hungary, but they were soon swept away. The Russian revolution would be forced to hold out alone for two decades, a prospect which neither Lenin nor Trotsky foresaw.

Above: A demonstration in Moscow, 1920. Placards show Lenin, Marx and Trotsky, but also (second portrait from the right) Karl Liebknecht, the German revolutionary leader who had been murdered by the Freikorps in January of the previous year following an abortive uprising in Berlin of the pro-Bolshevik wing of the German Socialist movement.

On 25 April 1920 Marshal Pilsudski, dictator of Poland, invaded the Ukraine. This attack was initially successful, and Pilsudski took Kiev (which now changed government for the fifteenth time since the revolution). On 12 June it was recaptured, and the Polish troops were soon in full flight.

Trotsky now urged that the Soviet offensive halt at the Polish border; to go further would alienate a people so recently escaped from Tsarist domination. But he was alone among the Russian leadership. Lenin believed that the Polish workers and peasants would greet the Red Army as their liberators.

More: a Soviet Poland would give the Russians access to the workers of Germany.

Trotsky accepted the majority decision and gave the order to march on Warsaw; but he did not visit the front. Far from igniting revolution, the invading army met with mounting hostility. Nevertheless Tukhachevsky was at the gates of Warsaw by mid-July, and there he waited for Voroshilov to join him from the south. But the latter, encouraged as ever by Stalin, sought instead to win glory through the conquest of Lvov. On 16 August Pilsudski attacked Tukhachevsky's southern flank, and forced him into headlong retreat.

An armistice was signed on 12 October, recognizing a frontier roughly along the historic border between the two countries. After the initial shock of defeat the majority of the Soviet Politburo, with Lenin among them, were soon arguing for a renewed offensive. Trotsky threatened to open a factional struggle among the party rank and file. Lenin relented, and peace was secured. So ended the first attempt to export revolution on the point of a bayonet.

Above: Poster by David Moor shows Trotsky crushing Polish reactionaries.
Opposite page: With E. M. Sklyansky.

Trotsky reviewing a military parade in Kiev.

OBIECALI BOLSZEWICY
DAMY WAM POKÓJ
DAMY WAM WOLNOŚĆ
DAMY WAM ZIEMIĘ,
PRACĘ I CHLEB -

NIKCZEMNIE OSZUKALI
ROZPĘTALI WOJNĘ,
Z POLSKĄ
ZAMIAST WOLNOŚCI DALI
PIĘŚĆ - ZAMIAST ZIEMI
- REKWIZYCJE
ZAMIAST PRACY - NĘDZĘ
ZAMIAST CHLEBA - GŁÓD

M. S. WOJSK. WYDZIAŁ PROPAGANDY

Above: A Polish propagandist resorts to anti-semitism to attack Trotsky. The poster accuses the Bolsheviks of betraying their own promises, bringing war instead of peace, repression instead of freedom, hunger instead of bread, and so on.

Opposite page: In similar vein, this White Russian poster depicts Trotsky as the ogre of the Kremlin. The heading reads: 'Peace and Freedom in Sovdepya' (a pejorative term for the Soviet Republic). Anti-Asiatic racism is also exploited here.

This painful step at least meant that he could no longer be accused of scheming to become the military dictator of the Soviet Union.

The Commissar of War poses with Red Army graduate officers in 1924. Trotsky resigned all his posts in the army on 15 January 1925.

advanced countries. Anyone who rejected this 'theory' was denounced for defeatism.

The official name for this campaign of vilification was the 'literary debate'. It culminated in January 1925, when a session of the Central Committee was convened to consider 'the Trotsky case'. He was obliged to resign from the Commissariat of War, and was warned not to engage in any new controversy, on pain of expulsion from the Central Committee. A directive was issued that the entire party membership should be 'enlightened' about the anti-Bolshevik character of Trotskyism.

Above: Red Week, 1924. From left to right are Voroshilov, Trotsky, Kalinin, Frunze (with Budienny above him) and the German revolutionary Clara Zetkin.

In late 1924 Stalin embarrassed even his own friends by announcing that he himself had led the October revolution, and that 'Trotsky did not and could not play any leading part'. The fabrications became even wilder, but their common core was their denunciation of 'Trotskyism', an alien, Menshevik heresy which was seeking to subvert Leninism and the revolution. Two years later, when Stalin had turned on his former colleagues in the troika, Zinoviev confessed: 'You must understand that it was a struggle for power. The trick was to string together the old disagreements with new issues. For this purpose "Trotskyism" was invented.' An equally important invention was Stalin's doctrine of 'Socialism in One Country', which flatly contradicted the entire canon of Marxist-Leninist thought. Stalin now announced that it was possible to build socialism in the Soviet Union alone, without the help of revolutionary régimes in more

На последнем пленуме вновь избранного ЦК РКП в члены политбюро избраны т. т. Л. Каменев, И. Сталин, Л. Троцкий, А. Рыков, Н. Бухарин, Г. Зиновьев, М. Томский.

Above: The Politbureau in 1924. Clockwise, from top left: Kamenev, Stalin, Trotsky, Tomsky, Zinoviev, Bukharin, Rykov. Below and opposite page: Trotsky reviews the troops in Red Square, 7 November 1924.

Following the Thirteenth Congress Trotsky was bound by party discipline not to reopen the debate on the economy and inner-party democracy. But during the summer of 1924 the State Publishing House, which was issuing his collected works in a many-volumed edition, was preparing his writings of 1917. Trotsky seized the opportunity to add an introduction entitled 'Lessons of October', a reference not only to the Bolshevik revolution but also to the third débâcle of the German revolution, an insurrection which had been planned for October 1923. Poorly prepared, the rising was called off at the last moment — and even that was bungled. The Hamburg Communists fought alone for several days before suffering inevitable defeat at the hands of the army.

'Lessons of October' exposed the roles during 1917 of Zinoviev, Kamenev and indeed the entire Bolshevik leadership, who had stumbled from equivocation to compromise in the absence of Lenin. 'Even within the Bolshevik Party, among its tops, on the eve of decisive action there was formed a group of experienced revolutionaries, old Bolsheviks who were in sharp opposition to the proletarian revolution and who, in the course of the most critical period of the revolution from February 1917 to approximately February 1918, adopted on all fundamental questions an essentially social-democratic position ... This must never be forgotten if we wish other Communist parties to learn anything from us.'

The publication of these unwelcome reminders of the past unleashed, perhaps predictably, a tornado of resentment against the parvenu, the ex-Menshevik who had joined the party only in August 1917, and had immediately eclipsed them all. Trotsky's revelations had to be discredited at all cost.

Trotsky, meanwhile, was suffering another attack of malaria. Natalya remembered: 'The second attack of L.D.'s illness coincided with a monstrous campaign of persecution against him, which we felt as keenly as if we had been suffering from the most malignant disease. The pages of "Pravda" seemed endless, and every line of the paper, even every word, a lie. L.D. kept silent. But what it cost him to maintain that silence! I remember that someone once asked him if he had read that day's paper. He replied that he no longer read the newspapers ... To read the papers at that time was exactly, he would say, like pushing a chimney brush down one's own throat.'

174

Trotsky at a gathering in the Caucasus, 1924, of Civil War veterans, still fiercely loyal to the founder of the Red Army.

Convalescence at Sukhum in the Caucasus, 1924. In the picture above left, Trotsky and Natalya, surrounded by aides, honour a local dignitary. Above, the patient takes gentle exercise. Far left, the seaside rest-home where Trotsky spent several months recuperating from influenza, catarrh, bronchitis, persistent fever and loss of weight and appetite. Left, the patient, evidently somewhat recovered, takes the opportunity to do a little shooting under the supervision of his doctor (the man standing between Trotsky and Natalya in the nearest photograph).

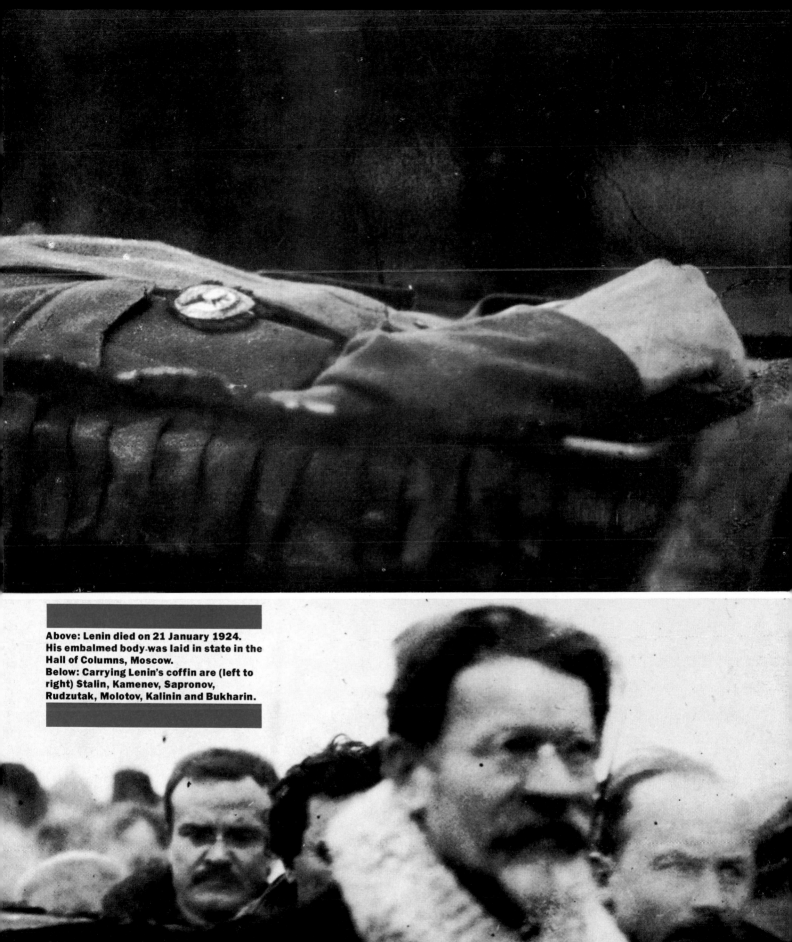

Above: Lenin died on 21 January 1924.
His embalmed body was laid in state in the
Hall of Columns, Moscow.
Below: Carrying Lenin's coffin are (left to
right) Stalin, Kamenev, Sapronov,
Rudzutak, Molotov, Kalinin and Bukharin.

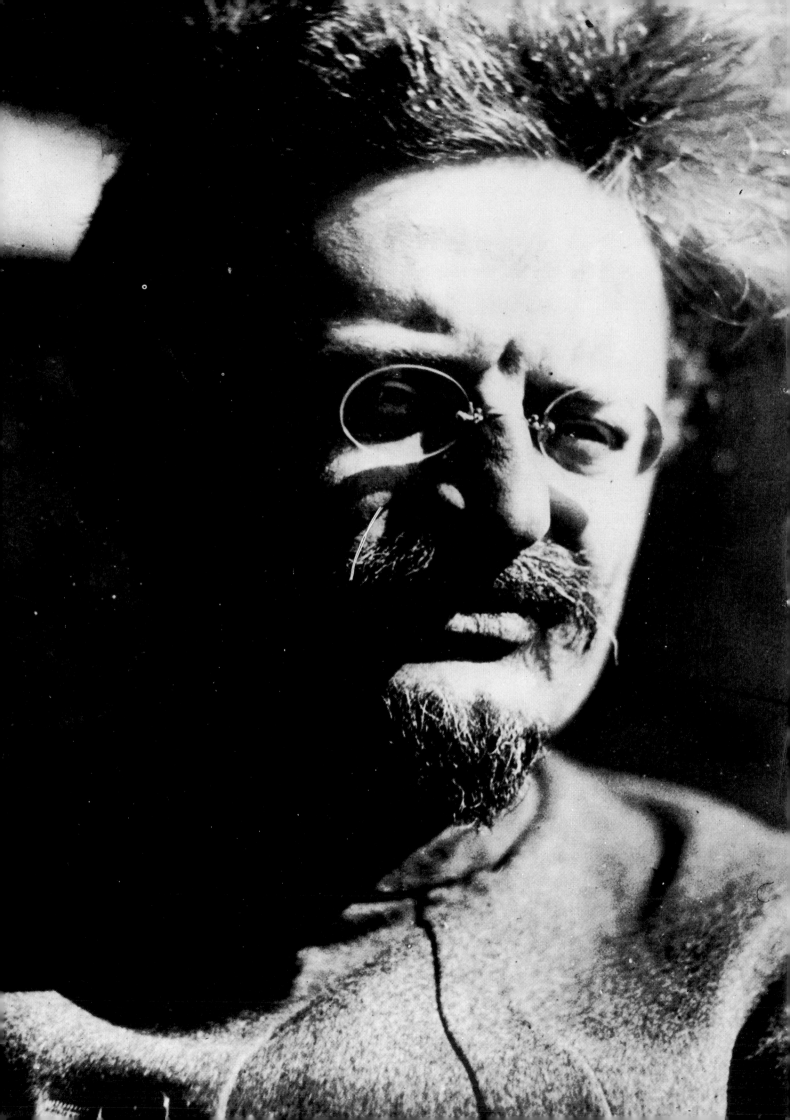

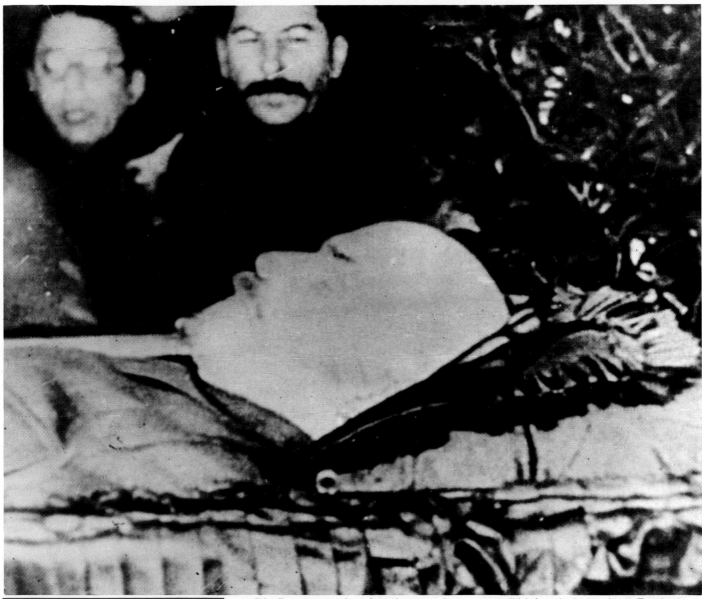

On 21 January 1924 Trotsky was in Tiflis, travelling to a sanatorium in Sukhum on the Black Sea, when a telegram arrived from Stalin saying that Lenin had died. Trotsky did not attend the funeral because Stalin misled him about the date. But from his bed he wrote a moving appreciation of the only man whom he had recognized as his superior. In return Krupskaya wrote a tender note: 'The attitude of V.I. towards you at the time when you came to us in London from Siberia has not changed until his death. I wish you, Lev Davidovich, strength and health, and I embrace you warmly.'

The troika moved fast. They promoted the pliable Rykov to replace Lenin. And they announced the 'Lenin levy', a vast recruitment drive which brought a quarter of a million politically green workers into the party between February and May. In this way they hoped to smother the opposition.

Krupskaya had kept Lenin's testament under lock and key until he died. Now she was demanding that the party be told what it contained. On 22 May the Central Committee met on the eve of the Thirteenth Party Congress to hear the will. Stalin's luck seemed to have run out at last. But Zinoviev and Kamenev pleaded that Lenin's criticism of Stalin was exaggerated; and it was decided not to publish the will. (In fact it was not made public in the USSR until 1956.) Trotsky sat silent throughout the meeting, merely indicating his disgust in gestures.

The Thirteenth Congress duly pronounced anathema on Trotsky. Zinoviev declared that 'It is now a thousand times more necessary than ever that the party should be monolithic,' and tried to force Trotsky to recant his views. Trotsky replied:

'Comrades, none of us wishes to be or can be right against the party. In the last instance the party is always right, because it is the only historic instrument which the working class possesses for its fundamental tasks. Nothing could be easier than to say before the party that all these criticisms and all these declarations, warnings and protests were mistaken from beginning to end. I cannot say so, however, because, comrades, I do not think so.'

Above: Stalin contemplates Lenin's corpse. Opposite page: Trotsky convalescing at the Black Sea resort of Sukhum.

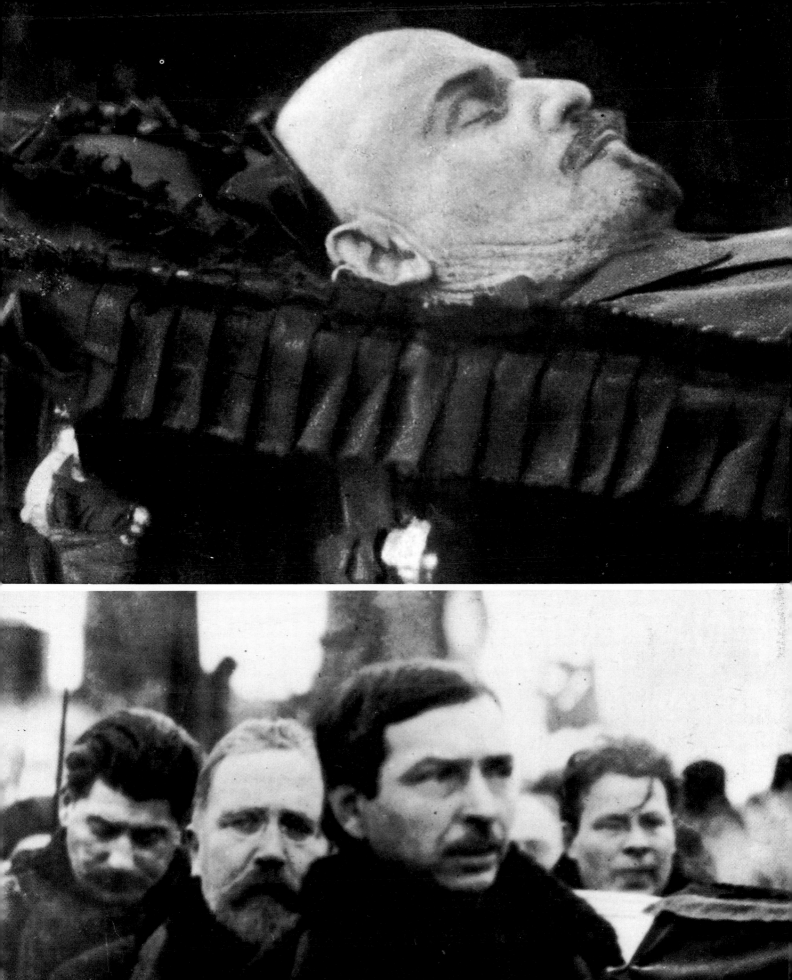

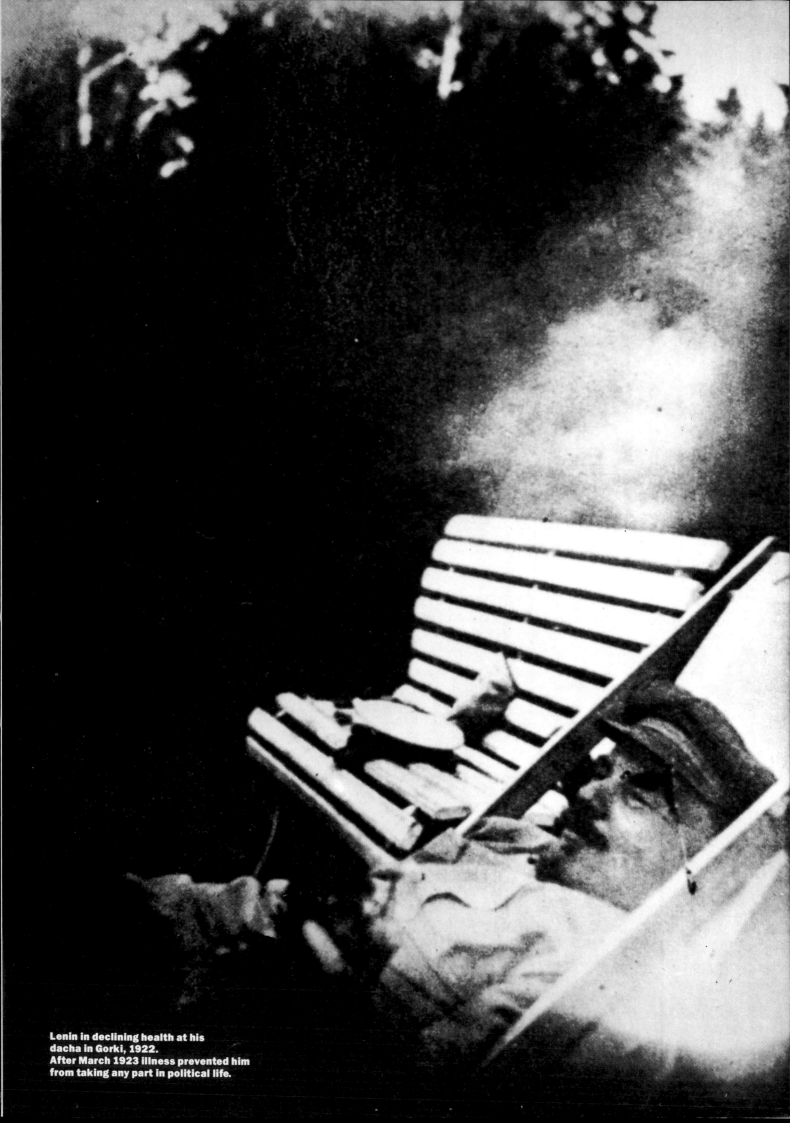

Lenin in declining health at his
dacha in Gorki, 1922.
After March 1923 illness prevented him
from taking any part in political life.

At the end of October 1923, while on a hunting trip, Trotsky contracted malaria and was condemned to inactivity for several months. But he was not altogether silent. Beginning in early December, he published a series of articles in 'Pravda' warning of the dangers of bureaucracy:

'The maintenance of the unity of the party is the gravest concern of the great majority of Communists. But it must be said openly: If there is today a serious danger to the unity or at the very least to the unanimity of the party, it is unbridled bureaucratism. This is the camp in which provocative voices have been raised. That is where they have dared to say: We are not afraid of a split! It is the representatives of this tendency who thumb through the past, seeking out everything likely to inject more rancour into the discussion, resuscitating artificially the recollections of the old struggle and the old split in order to accustom imperceptibly the mind of the party to the possibility of a crime as monstrous and as disastrous as a new split.' He spoke of 'bureaucratic degeneration', and drew comparisons with the evolution of the old socialist leaders towards reformism. The party, he said, must 'replace the mummified bureaucrats with fresh elements'.

Pandemonium broke loose in the party. Oppositionists saw in Trotsky's articles confirmation of all they had been saying; others felt he was stabbing the party in the back. Preparations were then underway for a national party conference, scheduled for January 1924, and the troika exploited the opportunity to tarnish Trotsky's name while he was incapacitated. The conference itself was packed with Stalin's appointees, and declared Trotsky and the 'forty-six' guilty of 'petty-bourgeois deviations'.

'Five years of Soviet power'.
Trotsky addresses demonstrators in
Red Square, 7 November 1922.

Lenin now knew he had very little time left. The Communist régime no longer had any external enemies to fear, but there was every sign that the party itself could split. Between 23 and 31 December 1922 he dictated a series of notes, intended for publication after his death, known as the 'Testament'. On the 24th he wrote:

'The prime factors in the question of stability are such members of the CC as Stalin and Trotsky. I think relations between them make up the greater part of the danger of a split ... Comrade Stalin, having become general secretary, has unlimited authority concentrated in his hands, and I am not sure whether he will always be capable of using that authority with sufficient caution. Comrade Trotsky, on the other hand, as his struggle against the CC on the question of the People's Commissariat for Communications

160

has already proved, is distinguished not only by outstanding ability. He is personally perhaps the most capable man in the present CC, but he has displayed excessive preoccupation with the purely administrative side of the work ...

'I shall not give any further appraisals of the personal qualities of other members of the CC. I shall just recall that the October episode with Zinoviev and Kamenev was, of course, no accident, but neither can the blame for it be laid upon them personally, any more than non-Bolshevism can upon Trotsky.'

The references to the People's Commissariat for Communications and to Trotsky's preoccupation with administration allude to the controversy over the role of trade unions. The 'October episode' was, of course, the Bolshevik Revolution — and Kamenev's and Zinoviev's opposition to it.

The most surprising feature of the Testa-

ment so far is that Stalin should have been treated as Trotsky's equal. Stalin had not been a prominent member of the leadership, and he was certainly no theoretician. But Lenin was now aware — as Trotsky was not — that the General Secretary was a formidable figure. Lenin's objective was to bridle both Stalin and Trotsky so that they could remain CC members without provoking a potentially disastrous split.

By the 30th his attitude had decisively changed. He apologized to the workers of Russia for failing to pay attention to the position of the nationalities in the new republic. Gross errors had been made. 'The political responsibility for all this truly Great Russian nationalist campaign must, of course, be laid on Stalin and Dzerzhinsky.' (The latter was head of the secret police, the Cheka.)

Now all ideas of mediating between Trotsky and Stalin were set aside. On 4 January Lenin wrote: 'Stalin is too rude and this defect, although quite tolerable in our midst and in dealings among us Communists, becomes intolerable in a general secretary. That is why I suggest that the comrades think about a way of removing Stalin from that post and appointing another man in his stead who in all other respects differs from Comrade Stalin in having only one advantage, namely that of being more tolerant, more loyal, more polite, and more considerate to the comrades, less capricious, etc.'

In January and February, struggling with his deteriorating health, Lenin dictated five articles on the subject of bureaucracy. Astonishingly, Stalin and his supporters contemplated printing a special issue of 'Pravda', consisting of one copy, containing Lenin's article on Rabkrin, and giving that to the old man — but Trotsky foiled the plan. At the beginning of March a secret commission reported to Lenin on the entire Georgian affair. He wrote to the Georgian Communists, Stalin's opponents, promising his full support, and to Trotsky:

'I earnestly ask you to undertake the defence of the Georgian affair at the Central Committee of the Party. That affair is now under "persecution" at the hands of Stalin and Dzerzhinsky and I cannot rely on their impartiality. Indeed, quite the contrary! If you would agree to undertake its defence, I could be at rest.' He added that under no circumstances should Trotsky accept a 'rotten compromise' from Stalin.

Trotsky, somewhat surprised at Lenin's change of heart on an issue which had been contentious between them, asked one of Lenin's secretaries for an explanation. She replied that 'it is probably because Vladimir Ilyich is getting worse and is in a hurry to do what he can'. The following day Lenin wrote to Stalin, breaking off all personal relations because of the latter's contemptuous behaviour towards Krupskaya. He also told another secretary that he was preparing a 'bomb' against Stalin, and that he intended to 'crush him politically'. But on the 7th he suffered another stroke, and on the 10th was again paralysed and lost the power of speech. He never recovered. He remained a silent witness to the developing power struggle until he died eleven months later, on 21 January 1924.

Top: Stalin with Felix Dzerzhinsky.
Above: Trotsky engaged in committee work. He argued insistently for a unified plan to tackle the country's economic problems.
Left: Nadezhda Krupskaya, Lenin's wife. Stalin threatened to prosecute her for writing a letter at her husband's request.
Opposite page: Trotsky with Christian Rakovsky. Rakovsky, since January 1919 President of the Ukrainian Soviet Republic, led the opposition to Stalin's 'imperialistic' national policy. In July 1923 he was posted as Soviet ambassador to Britain.

The Twelfth Party Congress was scheduled for April 1923. Stalin knew that Trotsky was in possession of a dossier from Lenin (the 'bomb') on the Georgian affair, and he was desperate that its contents be hidden from the party membership. He sent Kamenev to negotiate a deal.

Trotsky accepted a compromise — and it proved every bit as rotten as Lenin had predicted. Trotsky demanded 'a radical change in the policy on the national question, a discontinuation of persecutions of the Georgian opponents of Stalin, a discontinuation of the administrative oppression of the party, a firmer policy in matters of industrialization, and an honest cooperation in the higher centres'. In return Trotsky would not insist on Stalin's removal. Stalin leapt at the deal.

At the congress Trotsky sat silently as Stalin delivered his report on the national question. The Georgian delegates were mortified — Lenin's promised support did not materialize. Trotsky spoke only on economic issues, which he clearly considered fundamental to the survival of the revolutionary state. Meanwhile Stalin, Zinoviev and Kamenev — the 'troika' or triumvirate — presented themselves openly as the collective leadership of the party. They attracted considerable criticism, much of which echoed Trotsky's own views, but he offered the critics no backing. He seems to have been concerned, as Lenin had been, to discourage factional activity which could lead to a split in the party. And he had no intention of making a 'bid for power', especially as Lenin was still alive and might recover.

Stalin was not so squeamish. Throughout the summer of 1923 he consolidated his power base in the party, using his position as General Secretary to appoint amenable officials to key positions. In this way he gradually assumed the dominant position in the troika. Carefully avoiding any direct

Above: Felix Dzerzhinsky (left) and Gregory Ordzhonikidze. At the end of 1922 the latter had assaulted a Georgian Communist, Kabanidze, during an argument over Stalin's attitude to the national minorities. It was when he heard of this incident that Lenin decided to find out what Stalin and Dzerzhinsky were really up to in Georgia. Above right: Stalin, Rykov, Zinoviev and Bukharin — united in their opposition to Trotsky, who referred to them contemptuously as 'the epigones'.

attack on Trotsky, who was after all by far the most popular Communist leader after Lenin, he encouraged a whispering campaign against him, insinuating that the Red Army leader harboured ambitions to become the Bonaparte of the Russian Revolution. And, of course, he had no intention whatever of honouring his agreement with Trotsky.

In the summer strikes broke out in several major industries. While the rich peasants and newly arrived capitalist merchants (called Nepmen) prospered, the poor peasantry were less able than ever to afford industrial produce. In October a document appeared above the signature of forty-six leading

Bolsheviks, many of whom shared Trotsky's views. It demanded a shift in economic policy and a liberalization of the inner-party régime. Trotsky was coming into ever sharper conflict with the Stalin bloc as they chipped away at his position — in the same month he attempted in disgust to resign from every office he held, asking to be transferred to Germany where a new revolutionary crisis was simmering. But still he did not place himself at the head of the opposition. The 'forty-six' were shamelessly calumniated, and Trotsky himself was blamed for fomenting a split.

Trotsky reviewing a parade
of graduate officers in
Red Square, 10 January 1922.

Economic and administrative issues moved increasingly to the centre of Trotsky's attention during 1921 and 1922. He became convinced that it was necessary to formulate and carry through a national economic plan — an idea which, so soon after the introduction of NEP, struck most of the Communist leadership as perverse. Another conclusion which he reached was that the work of the state was being smothered by a monstrously inefficient bureaucracy. A Workers' and Peasants' Inspectorate, known as Rabkrin, had been created to supervise the work of the civil service, but Trotsky was scathing: 'In every branch of government it is well known that whenever the need arises for any change of policy or for any serious reform in organization it is useless to look to Rabkrin for guidance. Rabkrin itself provides striking illustration of the lack of correspondence between governmental decree and governmental machinery, and is itself becoming a powerful factor of muddle and wantonness.' The head of Rabkrin was Stalin.

Lenin did not at first accept Trotsky's arguments on the economy; and although he was acutely aware of the problem of bureaucracy, he attributed it to the legacy of Tsarism and capitalism. He complained at the Eleventh Party Congress in March 1922 that the machinery of the state 'was like a car that was going not in the direction the driver desired, but in the direction someone else desired; as if it were being driven by some mysterious, lawless hand, God knows whose, perhaps of a profiteer, or of a private capitalist, or of both'.

He was by no means an unqualified admirer of Stalin: when, a few days after this speech, Zinoviev proposed Stalin as General Secretary of the Party, Lenin turned to Trotsky and remarked: 'This cook will make only peppery dishes.' But he suspected that Trotsky's attacks were motivated by spite. He was also offended when, a week after Stalin's election, Trotsky flatly rejected the post of deputy head of state. There were already two other Vice-Premiers, and it looked as though Trotsky was too proud to acknowledge them as equals.

Lenin's health — like Trotsky's — had been poor for some time. On 25 May 1922 he suffered a stroke which left him partly paralysed and unable to speak; he did not return to work in the Kremlin until 2 October. Forced to observe events from afar, he became increasingly alarmed at the behaviour of the majority of Central Committee members. On issues of economic management he was coming to accept the force of Trotsky's arguments, and asked him to champion their common viewpoint.

Meanwhile Stalin was preparing a new constitution for the country. He proposed that the six national republics of the Soviet federation should be subordinated to Russia. This plan aroused fierce opposition, especially in Georgia, where Stalin and his deputies treated the local leadership as representatives of a conquered nation.

Lenin came to know of the row. He still trusted Stalin's assertion that the Georgians showed 'nationalist deviations': Stalin, as Commissar for Nationalities, should after all have known what he was talking about — and he was himself a Georgian. But his constitution was clearly unacceptable, and Lenin radically amended it. Stalin contemptuously accused Lenin of 'national liberalism' and rejected all his amendments. Then, having second thoughts, he accepted them, arguing that they were of small importance.

Above: During a remission in his illness, Lenin presides over a meeting of the Soviet of People's Commissars, October 1922. Trotsky is seated at the table, fourth from the right.
Opposite page: Stalin with Lenin at Gorki in August 1922. The Central Committee entrusted Stalin with the supervision of Lenin's medical treatment.

On 11 October Trotsky and Lenin held a long conversation on the subject of the bureaucracy. At the end of it they agreed to form a bloc against Stalin and his Organizational Bureau, and arranged to discuss the matter again.

On 13 December Lenin suffered two dangerous strokes, followed by a brief remission. On the 22nd Stalin, now confident that Lenin would not return to political life, violently abused Krupskaya for having written a letter, dictated by Lenin, congratulating Trotsky for having successfully defended their common viewpoint on economic questions. That night Lenin was again paralysed.

The war now over, Trotsky took up permanent residence in the Kremlin with Natalya, Lyova and Sergei. Lenin and Krupskaya lived along the corridor, and the two families shared a dining-room and bathroom.

Natalya headed the Arts Department of the Commissariat of Education. Trotsky remained Commissar of War, and still delivered the stirring orations at army rallies, but more often nowadays he wore civilian clothes. He turned his attention to international issues, and along with Lenin reorientated the Communist International away from Bukharin's 'theory of the offensive' and towards the tactic of the united front: Communists, in most countries a large minority of the working class, should seek limited agreements with the reformists in defence of working-class interests. Trotsky explained: 'It is precisely in the course of struggle that broad masses must learn from experience that we fight better than the others, that we see more clearly than the others, that we are more audacious and resolute. In this way we shall bring closer the hour of the united revolutionary front under undisputed Communist leadership.'

Above: A film session in the Kremlin. Opposite page: Trotsky entering his office in the Commissariat of War.

LEO D. TROTZKI

Das hungernde Russland und das satte Europa

DER MALIK-VERLAG/BERLIN

151

Above: Fragments of a film of Trotsky
speaking, c.1921.
Opposite page: A pamphlet by Trotsky on
the Russian famine published in Germany
by the recently founded left-wing
publishing house Malik Verlag, 1921.

workers themselves to barter for food. The black market traded openly in Moscow.

Internationally, too, the prospects of revolution were receding. This painful truth was underlined by the defeat in March 1921 of an ill-planned uprising in Germany which had been instigated from Moscow by Bukharin, Zinoviev and Radek. Soviet Russia was now obliged to negotiate for the 'normalization' of relations with other states, notably Britain. At home and abroad, these were times of forced retreat.

Above: After seven years of world war, revolution and civil war, famine devastated southern Russia in 1921.

The spring of 1921 brought ominous news of drought, sandstorms and a plague of locusts in the populous farmlands of the Volga region, south-east of Moscow. By the end of the year 36 million people were starving.

Multitudes drifted aimlessly across the vast plains. The Bolsheviks were forced to ask the imperialist nations for humanitarian aid.

Conditions in the cities were scarcely better. As the Civil War drew to an end Moscow had roughly half and Petrograd one third of their former populations. The workers who

remained had little or nothing to do because they lacked raw materials and parts. In 1921 Russia's industrial output was one fifth of the level of 1913; coal and iron production had virtually ceased; and the railway system had collapsed. Most of what was nevertheless produced in the cities was taken by the

Two cubo-futurist drawings of Trotsky by Yuri Annenkov.

Above: Trotsky (indicated by the arrow) arriving to review Red Army divisions before the counter-offensive was launched against Pilsudski's Poland in the summer of 1920. Left and right: A rousing speech for the departing troops. Yet Trotsky profoundly disagreed with the Red Army's invasion of Polish territory. He later wrote: 'We overestimated the revolutionary character of the Polish internal situation . . . In the great class war now taking place, military intervention from without can play but a concomitant, cooperative, secondary part. Military intervention may hasten the dénouement and make the victory easier, but only when both the political consciousness and the social conditions are ripe for revolution. Military intervention has the same effect as a doctor's forceps; if used at the right moment, it can shorten the pangs of birth, but if employed prematurely, it will merely cause an abortion.'

Lenin addressing a demonstration in Sverdlov Square, Moscow, 5 May 1920. Kamenev and Trotsky, on the podium steps, await their turn to speak. Notoriously, Stalin's propagandists later painted Trotsky out of this scene in their attempt to delete him from the history of the revolution.

This photograph was taken soon after the one on the previous page, but from the other side of the podium. Lenin and Kamenev have made their speeches and are now listening to Trotsky.

Trotsky, Lenin and Kamenev chatting after the Sverdlov Square rally.
Opposite page: A portrait of Trotsky in 1920 by the photographer Moisei Nappelbaum.

КОНТР-РЕВОЛЮЦИЯ

Above: A Civil War poster by Victor Deni
depicts Trotsky as Saint George slaying the
counter-revolutionary dragon. Early Soviet
propaganda frequently borrowed and
adapted Christian imagery and mythology
to put across a revolutionary message,
while in republics with predominantly
Moslem populations the red crescent was a
common motif in preference to the star.
Opposite page: The Second Congress of the
Communist International met in Petrograd
and Moscow in July and August 1920. Here
Trotsky is being filmed as he addresses a
demonstration in honour of the delegates.

Trotsky wrote the manifesto adopted by the
second Comintern congress, as he had done
for the first, and he delivered the
concluding speech. Alfred Rosmer later
recalled: 'The man, his words, the listening
crowd, all contributed to giving this final
session of the Congress a moving dignity.
The speech had lasted a little more than
an hour. Trotsky had spoken without notes;
it was wonderful . . . to watch the
passionate intensity on the faces of those
following his speech.'
Left: A young army recruit has words with
the Commissar of War.

Leaders of the world revolution pictured
at the Second World Congress of the
Communist International, 1920. From left
to right: Giacinto Serrati of the Italian
Socialist Party, Trotsky, Alfred Rosmer
from France, Paul Levi from Germany,
Zinoviev (who was President
of the International) and Bukharin.
Opposite page: 'Leader of the Revolution!
General Trotsky', one of a series
of postcards produced by the German
Communist Party.

No. 4. RUSSLAND:
Führer der Revolution!
Gen. Trotzki.

Above: The satirical magazine 'Red Pepper'
introduces its readers to the Soviet United
soccer team.
In the front row are (left to right) Radek,
Sosnovsky, Trotsky, Riazanov and Bukharin,
and behind them Zinoviev, Lenin, Marx
(who has possession of the ball), Kamenev,
Lozovsky and Chicherin.
Left: Trotsky at a demonstration
in Red Square, 1920, with his sons Sergei
and Lyova (facing the camera).
Opposite page: Trotsky in conversation
with E.M. Sklyansky (his deputy at
the People's Commissariat of War) and
General S. Kamenev after the speech we saw
being filmed on page 120.

тов. Тёмкин.
тов. Петерсон.
тов. Коллонтай.
тов. Шмидт
тов. Надежный
тов. Енукидзе
тов. Иоффе
тов. Карахан
тов. Стеклов
тов. Каменев
тов. Ленин
тов. Калинин
тов. Троцкий
тов. Луначарский
тов. Рыков
тов. Зиновьев
тов. Демьян-Бедный
тов. Христинский
тов. Рыков
Красная Москва
тов. Чичерин
тов. Курский
тов. Бухарин

Above: 'A gift to young artists'. The revolutionary holidays are coming round again, bringing the usual heavy demand for portraits of the Soviet leaders. 'Red Pepper' offers helpful hints for the mass production of such portraits. Starting with the blank face (no. 1) and adding the appropriate accessories, in no time a variety of identikit celebrities can be turned out. By way of demonstration we are shown Lenin (no. 2), Kalinin (4), Radek (8), Trotsky (11), Marx (13) and a newly created synthesis awaiting designation (17). Such portraits, 'Red Pepper' assures us, will be guaranteed a place in all serious publications provided that the artist remembers to state clearly the name of the person portrayed and explains that it has come 'from So-and-So's private collection'. Grateful artists are invited to call at the 'Red Pepper' offices any afternoon between 3 and 5 to offer their thanks. Satire at the expense of the Bolshevik leaders was commonplace in the early 1920s — and unthinkable by the end of the decade.

Opposite page: A contemporary composite showing Red Moscow and many of its leading figures. Kalinin is in the centre of the picture, flanked by Lenin and Trotsky; Radek is third up on the right.

Trotsky addressing a meeting in Red Square, 1920.

Above: In the autumn of 1920 the English sculptor Claire Sheridan visited Moscow to make busts of the Bolshevik leaders. A woman of aristocratic family (she was a cousin of Winston Churchill) and romantic temperament, she saw Civil War Russia from a somewhat odd perspective. At first Trotsky refused to see her, but then he relented. She remembered their first sitting, in Trotsky's office at the Commissariat of War: 'My heart sank at the difficulties of the situation. I looked at my man, who was bending down, writing at his desk. Impossible to see his face. I looked at him and then at my clay, in despair. Then I went and knelt in front of the writing table opposite him, with my chin on his papers. He looked up from his writing and stared back, a perfectly steady, unabashed stare. His look was a solemn, analytical one, perhaps mine was too. After a few seconds, realizing the absurdity of our attitudes, I had to laugh and said: "I hope you don't mind being looked at." "I don't mind," he said. "I have my *revanche* in looking at you, and it is I who gain."' From this photograph it seems that the experience permanently shaped her attitude to the People's Commissar.

Opposite page: A studio photograph of Trotsky in a more approachable mood, taken during the same period.

Л. Д. Троцкий.

In the winter of 1919–20, as the pace of the Civil War slackened, Trotsky was in the Urals attempting to reconstruct the ravaged economy — or at any rate to arrest its further decline. Industrial production was at a fraction of its pre-war level. As for the railways, it was possible to predict mathematically their complete extinction by mid-1920 unless something was done.

Inflation had rendered the currency worthless and, especially in the countryside, commerce was replaced by barter. The free market in food was officially abolished and replaced by a systematic policy of requisitioning. This measure had been forced on the Soviet government as a result of the war. While there remained a danger that the Whites would return and repossess their estates, the peasants on the whole considered requisitioning a lesser evil. But as the war drew to a close, peasant discontent was bound to grow. Meanwhile, agricultural output steadily declined.

Trotsky's solution was twofold: first, requisitioning should be replaced by a progressive income tax (in kind) and the provision of industrial products in proportion to the amount of grain supplied; and second, industrial production should be increased through the application of military discipline to the factories.

In those days the system of War Communism, as the current economic measures were known, was generally considered to be a bold step on the straight road to a classless society. Bukharin published an influential book entitled 'The Economics of the Transformation Period' which attempted to give theoretical justification to the system. It was not surprising, then, that the Central Committee rejected the first half of Trotsky's economic proposals — relating to agriculture — in February 1920, since he seemed to be advocating a dangerous concession to the peasantry. But his second idea met with Lenin's approval, at any rate so far as it meant converting the Red Army into a labour army. Steps were taken in this direction.

Trotsky did not pursue his argument for a more liberal treatment of the peasantry. However he did hammer home his demand that the trade unions be militarized — used to discipline the workers in the interest of increased production. But the workers, too, were tired of the war and its demands. A storm of protest gathered over Trotsky's head. He persisted, and the argument dragged on throughout 1920, earning him many enemies.

Above: Images of Trotsky were often associated at this time with industrialization and modernity, as in this stage set designed by Liubov Popova for Vsevolod Meyerhold's production of the play 'Zemlya Dybom' ('Earth in Turmoil') by Sergei Tretyakov. In the centre the Tsar and his generals are shown upside down and symbolically 'deleted' from society. This production, staged in 1923, was dedicated to the Red Army and to Trotsky personally. Trotsky himself, while not opposed to innovation in the arts, was critical of the consciously 'proletarian' current in art which Tretyakov, among others, championed. 'The proletariat in bourgeois society', he said, 'is a propertyless and deprived class, and so it cannot create a culture of its own. Only after taking power does it really become aware of its own frightful cultural backwardness. In order to overcome this it needs to abolish those conditions which keep it in the position of a class, the proletariat. The more we can speak of a new culture in being, the less this will possess a class character.' He was also emphatic that the state, while clearly not indifferent to the political content of art, should be extremely careful in its interventions into cultural affairs.
Opposite page: From a series of sixty-one portraits of Bolshevik leaders.

Above: A portrait of Trotsky as Red Army commander by Yuri Annenkov. This painting was shown among the Russian exhibits at the Venice Bienniale in 1924, but has not been seen since.
Opposite page: The artist with his subject. Annenkov was best known in the Soviet Union for his collaboration with Nathan Altman and others in staging 'The Storming of the Winter Palace', a reenactment of the original event in Uritsky Square on 7 November 1920. The entire square was the stage, and there was a cast of thousands including a Red Army battalion, plus armoured cars, borrowed (without permission) for the occasion.

Above: A Red Army soldier is killed during the assault on Kronstadt naval base, which mutinied against the Bolsheviks in March 1921. Trotsky had remarked that it had been necessary to 'plunder all Russia' during the Civil War. The Kronstadt sailors, who had been recruited mainly from the Ukraine, expressed the demands of the peasantry for an end to War Communism. But they also won the support of many local Communists and almost the entire working-class population of the island on which they were based.
Far left: Troops loyal to the government in action against the Kronstadt sailors.
Left: M. N. Tukhachevsky, who commanded the Red Army forces in battle against the mutineers.

At the end of 1920 peasant rebellions swept the country. As one peasant complained at the Eighth Congress of Soviets in December: 'The land belongs to us, but the bread from it is yours; the rivers belong to us, but the fish are yours; the forests belong to us, but the wood from them to you.'

Lenin could no longer ignore the crisis in agriculture. He proposed a return to the free market and the encouragement of petty capitalism in the countryside. These ideas, which became known as the New Economic Policy, were presented to the Tenth Party Congress in March 1921. But they were too late to avert a tragedy.

At the beginning of March the sailors of Kronstadt, led by anarchists, rose in rebellion against the Soviet government. They were supported by strikes in nearby Petrograd. The insurgents demanded an end to requisitioning; freedom for all socialist parties (all but the Bolsheviks had by now been suppressed for counter-revolutionary activity); fresh elections to the Soviets; and lifting of the state of siege. They announced the beginning of the Third Revolution, against Bolshevik tyranny.

Spring was fast approaching, and the insurgents hoped to postpone a showdown until the ice surrounding their fortress had melted: then they would be virtually invincible. The Bolsheviks could not wait, and when their ultimatum to surrender was ignored they went into battle. Isaac Deutscher describes the scene:

'White sheets over their uniforms, the Bolshevik troops, under Tukhachevsky's command, advanced across the Bay of Finland. They were met by hurricane fire from Kronstadt's bastions. The ice broke under their feet, and wave after wave of white-shrouded attackers collapsed into the glacial Valhalla ... On 17 March, after a night-long advance in a snowstorm, the Bolsheviks at last succeeded in climbing the walls. When they broke into the fortress, they fell upon its defenders like revengeful furies.'

Trotsky was not present when the final assault took place. But the stigma of the Kronstadt tragedy clung to him because he was supreme military commander, because he defended the government's actions — and because, ever since the early days of the revolution, the sailors of Kronstadt had looked to him as their champion.

The New Economic Policy satisfied one half of the insurgents' demands; but as for democracy — the Tenth Congress refused elections. Further, the delegates feared that economic liberalization would lead to increased dangers of political fragmentation within the Communist Party itself. Factions were banned. At first this was considered a temporary, emergency measure; but it proved to be irreversible.

138

Above: Lenin and Trotsky surrounded by delegates to the Tenth Party Congress who had volunteered to join in the assault on Kronstadt, March 1921.
Left: Grigori Zinoviev, President of the Petrograd Soviet. Trotsky maintained that immediate political responsibility for the anti-Bolshevik revolt in Kronstadt and Petrograd lay with Zinoviev, who had demagogically aroused the expectations of the workers in his area — at the expense of Trotsky's popularity — during the debate on the role of trade unions.
Opposite page: Trotsky in 1921.

VI
СТРОИМ
И
ЗАВОЕВЫВАЕМ
ТЕХНИКУ

ДА ЗДРАВСТВУЕТ ВСЕМИРНАЯ РЕВОЛЮЦИЯ

Above and opposite page: The enthusiasm for organization, mechanization and 'American' methods which swept Soviet Russia in the first years after the Bolshevik revolution found powerful expression in the revolutionary visual technique of photomontage. The Red Army had provided the impetus for industrial innovation during the Civil War as well as consuming most of its product, and so was naturally taken as a symbol of modernity. In the photomontage opposite, by Alexander Rodchenko, Trotsky is seen speaking from the armoured train 'Guard of the Revolution'.

The architect of the Red Army's victories takes the salute in Red Square, 12 September 1921.

THE CONSPIRACY OF THE EPIGONES

SOVIET UNION 1921-1929

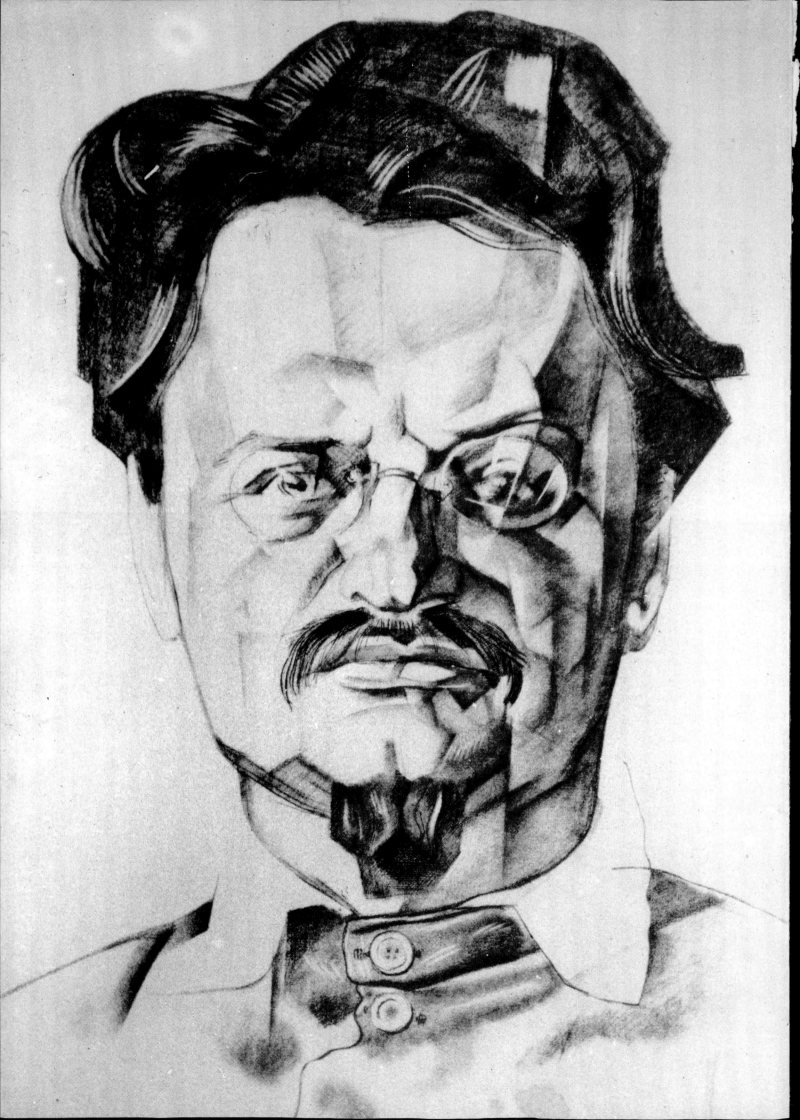

Л. ТРОЦКИЙ

КУДА ИДЕТ АНГЛИЯ?

ГОСУДАРСТВЕННОЕ
ИЗДАТЕЛЬСТВО
1925

LEO TROTZKI

WOHIN TREIBT ENGLAND?

Deutsche Verlagsgesellschaft für
Politik und Geschichte m.b.H.
BERLIN

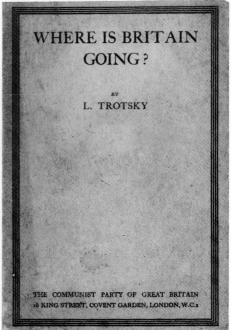

WHERE IS BRITAIN GOING?

BY
L. TROTSKY

THE COMMUNIST PARTY OF GREAT BRITAIN
16 KING STREET, COVENT GARDEN, LONDON, W.C.2

For a year and a half Trotsky and his followers on the left refrained from open opposition. He was given 'safe' jobs, mostly in economic development. He was largely responsible for the construction of the mammoth Dnieper hydro-electric dam system. He wrote 'Where is Britain Going?', predicting a great crisis a year before the General Strike and warning against reliance on the trade union leaders.

Stalin, emboldened by the quiescence of the left, now prepared to turn against Zinoviev and Kamenev. He formed a new alliance with Bukharin. The latter, once the far-left theoretician of War Communism, now announced that the Soviet Union would advance towards socialism 'at a snail's pace', and called to the kulaks (wealthy peasants), 'Enrich yourselves!' This they were already doing, largely at the expense of the workers.

In the summer of 1926, in the face of protests from some of his own supporters, Trotsky formed a Joint Opposition with Zinoviev and Kamenev. They demanded democracy within the party, improvements in wages and conditions for workers, and a real plan for industrialization. In retaliation Stalin had Zinoviev expelled from the Politbureau, and many less prominent oppositionists were victimized. Trotsky himself was hauled before a disciplinary committee.

Top: 'Where is Britain Going?' in Russian, German and English editions.
Above: A. B. Swales, President of the British TUC, enjoying the hospitality of Soviet trade unionists, 10 February 1926.
Opposite page: Trotsky in 1925.

Left: Voroshilov is speaking at Felix Dzerzhinsky's funeral, July 1926. To the right of him are Stalin (in white) and Rykov. On the far left, Trotsky (also in white) and, next to him, Zinoviev wait to speak.
Below left: Trotsky (centre left) and Stalin (fourth from right) accompany the coffin.
Below: Felix Dzerzhinsky, first head of the GPU. 'I am not a bad revolutionary, perhaps,' he would say of himself, 'but I am no leader.' At one time he had been a devoted follower of Trotsky, but he later attached himself to Stalin and defended all his actions with passionate intensity.

183

Felix Dzerzhinsky, a Polish revolutionary of long standing, had been appointed by Lenin to head the secret police, the Cheka (from 1923 called the GPU). He was chosen for the job because of his almost saintly asceticism, self-denial and sensitivity. He was extremely intense and emotionally volatile.

When the Central Committee met in July 1926 Trotsky delivered an attack on the foreign policy of the Stalin – Bukharin group, particularly their handling of affairs in Britain. They had tied Soviet policy to support for the Anglo-Russian Committee, a pact between the trade union leaders of the two countries. Even when the General Council of the TUC called off the General Strike, the Soviet leadership did not repudiate them. This episode, Trotsky argued, showed vividly how Stalin and Bukharin had abandoned revolutionary politics.

There was nothing especially new in these criticisms, but they provoked a violent reaction in Dzerzhinsky. For two hours, almost screaming, he denounced the Opposition in his high-pitched voice. As he stepped from the rostrum he suffered a heart attack and collapsed in front of the committee. He died the same day.

Trotsky and Stalin carrying Dzerzhinsky's coffin, Moscow, July 1926. Kalinin is in the foreground, Kamenev can be seen between Trotsky and

Stalin, and Bukharin is on the far right. This was Trotsky's last appearance in the Soviet Union as a leading member of the Communist Party.

Another major controversy arose over the Communist International's policy towards China. Against their better judgement, the Chinese Communists were instructed to join the Kuomintang, Chiang Kai-Shek's bourgeois nationalist movement. Trotsky's repeated protests against this policy were ignored. In April 1927 Chiang Kai-Shek's army turned on the Communists in their stronghold of Shanghai and massacred them. Stalin, however, saw no reason to alter his policy.

In September the Joint Opposition published their Platform in preparation for the Fifteenth Party Congress. It was suppressed, and the printers were arrested. Trotsky was expelled from the Executive Committee of the Communist International.

Stalin, still nervous that the Opposition's demands would find sympathy among the working class, suddenly announced that as part of the tenth anniversary celebrations of the October Revolution all workers would be granted a seven-hour day and five-day week with no loss of earnings. It is doubtful

whether anyone believed him. On the anniversary itself Oppositionists demonstrated in Leningrad, Moscow and elsewhere, as the French revolutionary Victor Serge relates: 'Chinese students of Moscow's Sun Yat-Sen University ... formed a long, sinuous dragon. In the middle of Red Square they threw Trotsky's proclamations in the air.' But Stalin's police retaliated ruthlessly, and as Trotsky himself tried to address a crowd a revolver shot was fired at him, hitting his car.

Above: The principal leaders of the Left Opposition in 1927. From left to right: front row, Leonid Serebriakov, Karl Radek, Trotsky, Mikhail Boguslavsky and Evgenii Preobrazhensky; standing, Christian Rakovsky, Yakov Drobnis, Alexander Beloborodov and Lev Sosnovsky. All of these men had been leading figures in the revolutionary movement since before 1917; besides Trotsky himself, Radek, Preobrazhensky and Rakovsky in particular had been well-known in the international Communist movement. But their association with the Left Opposition, however brief, cost them all their lives within the next few years.
Right: A postcard published in 1928 depicting the leaders of the revolution. Trotsky has not yet been quite expunged from history: he is squeezed in behind Stalin, next to the red flag.
Opposite page: Stalin's policies led to disaster in Britain, China and elsewhere, but reverses for the revolutionary movement only strengthened his own position, internationally as at home.

КРОКОДИЛ

Цена 15 коп.

№ 44

ГОД ИЗДАНИЯ ШЕСТОЙ

МОСКВА, НОЯБРЬ 1927 г.

НАДОЕЛА ЭТА МУЗЫКА!

— Играем, играем, а ни кто к нам не идет!..

The satirical review 'Krokodil' (November 1927) carries cartoons by Eliseev ridiculing Trotsky, Zinoviev and Kamenev. On the left Trotsky

НЕОПРОВЕРЖИМОЕ ДОКАЗАТЕЛЬСТВО

Рис. К. Елисеева

is the organ-grinder. Zinoviev the chanteuse is complaining: 'We play and play, but nobody pays any attention to us!' Kamenev is the parrot.

СAM *(глава семьи):*—Мы были правы,—яблоки нам бросали гнилые, калоши рваные... А что из этого следует? Что материальное положение рабочего класса тяжело,—как мы и говорили.

A group of Left Oppositionists in Moscow, 1927.
To the left of Trotsky is Ivan Smirnov, whom Lenin
had once described as 'the conscience of the
Party', and to the right is Ivan Smilga.
Standing second from the left is Man Nevelson,
husband of Trotsky's daughter Nina.

On 14 November 1927 Trotsky and Zinoviev were expelled from the Communist Party. Two days later Adolf Yoffe committed suicide. A friend and collaborator of Trotsky's since the days of the Vienna 'Pravda', he had been ill for some time. Now he wrote:

'You and I, dear Lev Davidovich, are bound to each other by decades of joint work, and, I make bold to hope, of personal friendship. This gives me the right to tell you in parting what I think you are mistaken in. I have never doubted the rightness of the road you pointed out ... But I have always believed that you lacked Lenin's unbending will, his unwillingness to yield, his readiness even to remain alone on the path that he thought right in the anticipation of a future majority ... Politically you were always right, beginning with 1905, and I told you repeatedly that with my own ears I had heard Lenin admit that even in 1905, you, and not he, were right. One does not lie before his death, and now I repeat this again to you ... But you have often abandoned your rightness for the sake of an overvalued agreement or compromise. This is a mistake. Don't lose your courage if someone leaves you now, or if not as many come to you, and not as soon, as we all would like ... Many a time I have wanted to tell you this, but only now have I brought myself to do so, as a last farewell.'

The authorities set Yoffe's funeral for 19 November, a working day, but 10,000 people joined the procession headed by Trotsky, singing revolutionary songs. At the graveside Trotsky spoke: 'Yoffe left us not because he did not wish to fight, but because he lacked the physical strength for fighting. He feared to become a burden on those engaged in struggle. His life, not his suicide, should serve as a model to those who are left behind. The struggle goes on. Everyone re-

mains at his post. Let nobody leave.'

This was Trotsky's last public appearance in Russia. Zinoviev and Kamenev, meanwhile, were desperate to 'leave their posts'. 'The time has come, Lev Davidovich, when we must have the courage to surrender,' they said, to which Trotsky scathingly replied, 'If this kind of courage, the courage to surrender, were all that was needed, the revolution should have been victorious by now the world over.' In December they recanted, and

2,500 of their followers deserted the Opposition with them. 1,500 party members who refused to submit were expelled and placed at the disposal of the secret police.

Above: Adolf Yoffe.
Opposite page: Trotsky with Yoffe (top) and at his funeral, 19 November 1927.

194

Cover by John Heartfield of the 'Illustrated History of the Russian Revolution', 1928. The photo on the front cover is of a pro-Bolshevik

195

march under attack in July 1917. The inclusion of Trotsky with Lenin (back cover) was by 1928 rare in official Communist publications.

The police announced that Trotsky and his family were to be deported to Alma Ata, in Central Asia, on 16 January 1928. A huge demonstration gathered at the station, so the authorities quickly postponed the journey for two days. But early the next morning they came and dragged him forcibly out of his apartment and bundled him, Natalya and Lyova — without hat, gloves or suitcases — onto the train. (Sergei remained in Moscow with his wife.) They reached their destination at 3 a.m. on the 25th. Voroshilov, Stalin's ally since the days of the Military Opposition, gloated: 'Even if he dies there, we won't hear of it in a hurry.'

But gradually Trotsky managed to re-establish contact with his supporters in the cities and in exile. His first wife, Alexandra, led the Oppositionists in Leningrad. Lyova was in charge of communications — his father appointed him 'Minister of Foreign Affairs' — and doubled up as bodyguard. A little money came in from translating and editing the works of Marx, commissions given to Trotsky by David Ryazanov, an old friend who was now Director of the Marx-Engels Institute in Moscow.

Across the vastness of Siberia came news of a new catastrophe. The kulaks refused to deliver bread at prices fixed by the state: emboldened by the Stalin—Bukharin régime's economic policies, they were making a 'bloodless uprising'. Soon Moscow was resorting to forcible requisitioning. Now Stalin turned on his erstwhile ally, having apparently discovered that Bukharin was the 'banner-bearer of capitalist restoration'. Rumours began to circulate that Trotsky was to be recalled and rehabilitated.

These developments disorientated many Trotskyists. It seemed that Stalin was now pursuing industrial and economic policies similar to those they had been advocating for years. The fact that he ruled the country through the ever more widespread use of terror did not deter Radek, Preobrazhensky, Pyatakov, Antonov-Ovseenko and hundreds of other Oppositionists from offering the General Secretary their support.

Radek's behaviour was particularly grotesque. After his capitulation he was taken to Moscow under GPU escort. During the journey he chanced to meet a group of loyal Oppositionists at a small station in Siberia. At once he began to abuse them, declaring that Trotsky was now his enemy. His guards dragged and kicked him, hysterically laughing, back into the train.

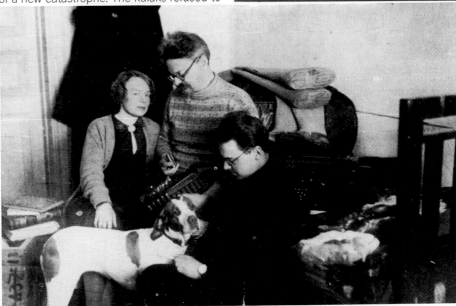

Above: Trotsky with Natalya and Lyova in exile at Alma Ata.
Right: Trotsky's daughter Nina. In spring 1928 news reached Alma Ata that her health had broken down following the deportation of her husband Man Nevelson. Trotsky spent anxious weeks waiting in vain for more information. She died on 9 June; only much later did he receive her last letter.
Left: Winter in Central Asia, 1928.

198 Despite the illusions created by Stalin's 'left turn', and despite the savagery of the repression against Oppositionists, the number of Trotsky's supporters continued to grow: by the end of 1928 the GPU had been obliged to imprison or deport roughly 8,000 of them. Stalin could not afford the risk represented by Trotsky's continued presence in the Soviet Union, and he was not yet confident enough to have him killed, so he decided to deport him. On 20 January 1929 troops surrounded and occupied the house at Alma Ata.

A harrowing journey began at dawn on the 22nd. 'The powerful tractor that was to tow us over the Kurday pass got lodged in the snow up to its neck, together with the seven automobiles it was towing. During the snowstorms seven men and a good many horses were frozen to death on the pass ... It took us more than seven days to advance about thirty kilometres.' Eventually they reached the railway. Their train set out for European Russia, then abruptly a telegram announced they were to be deported to Turkey. Trotsky refused to go voluntarily. 'Our train ... stops on a side-line near a dead little station and there sinks into a coma between two stretches of thin woods. Day after day goes by ... Waste ... Solitude ... Grippe rages in our car. We re-read Anatole France and Klyuchevsky's Russian history ... The cold reaches 53 degrees below zero F.'

After twelve days Stalin summoned the courage to proceed. They were taken to Odessa and put aboard the steamer 'Ilyich'. They landed in Constantinople on 12 February. The country they left behind was about to be plunged into horrors that even Trotsky did not foresee.

Above: Special edition of a Russian émigré publication on 'Trotsky and Trotskyists', January 1928.
Right: Left Oppositionists demonstrating in Siberia on the anniversary of the revolution, 1928. Their banners read: 'Turn the fire to the right, against kulak, Nepman and bureaucrat, not in words but in deeds' and 'Long live the dictatorship of the proletariat' (illustrated with portraits of Lenin and Trotsky).

Trotsky and Natalya are rushed by car to the Soviet Consulate in Constantinople, 12 February 1929

Zinoviev, Kamenev and Bukharin have
all been brought to heel; Trotsky has been
expelled from the country. Stalin is now
sole master of the Soviet Union. Here he is
pictured with his faithful follower
Ordzhonikidze among happy delegates to
the 1930 Party Congress, which voted
to 'Fulfil the Five-Year Plan in Four Years'.
This was 'the congress of the sweeping
offensive of Socialism along the
whole front', as Stalin announced 'to
hearty acclamation' (thus the official
record). Few of these smiling Stalinists
would survive the decade.

A propaganda float produced by the Academy of Artists, Sculptors and Caricaturists, Leningrad, 1930. Trotsky, carrying a briefcase labelled

'The "truth" about the USSR' (a reference to his anti-Stalinist writings published abroad), is running at the heels of world imperialism.

TURKEY, FRANCE, NORWAY 1929-1936

THE PLANET WITHOUT A VISA

Stalin was now master of the Soviet Union.
Exiled to Turkey, Trotsky (opposite page)
attempted to wrest the international Communist
movement from his adversary's hands.

Prinkipo Island, in the Sea of Marmara, was used in former centuries as a place of internment for opponents of the Byzantine Emperors. Trotsky and his household settled there in April 1929. He found that the islanders lived much as their forebears had done 1,000 years before; indeed 'the village cemetery seemed more alive than the village itself'. But he took full advantage of the opportunity to indulge his passion for fishing. He handled his hooks, lines and nets with the same meticulousness that he showed in his writing and political work.

For three weeks Trotsky and his family lived in the Soviet Consulate in Constantinople under the 'protection' of the GPU. The city was teeming with White Russian émigrés, and Turkey was ruled by the dictator Kemal Pasha (Ataturk), who was by no means a revolutionary communist.

The world's press buzzed with rumours about the destiny of the exiled revolutionary, but not a single country could be found to offer him asylum. Fortunately Kemal remembered with gratitude that Trotsky had supplied him with weapons during Turkey's war of independence, and treated his reluctant guest honourably. Meanwhile Trotsky set about contacting friends and sympathizers in Europe while Natalya and Lyova, trailing GPU men behind them, hunted for a house. At the end of April they settled on Prinkipo, 'a red-cliffed island set in deep blue', Trotsky wrote, crouched in the Sea of Marmara 'like a prehistoric animal drinking'.

Here they were scarcely at the centre of the world, but they were free. Friends and disciples began to arrive: Alfred and Marguerite Rosmer, comrades since the First World War and now leading oppositionists in Paris; Maurice and Magdeleine Paz, also from Paris; and younger activists from France, Germany and Czechoslovakia. A secretariat and bodyguard were organized, and Trotsky set to work.

The bulk of his writing was devoted to establishing the truth about the revolution and his own role in it. He finished 'My Life: An Attempt at an Autobiography', in which he demonstrated his literary as well as his polemical skills. Next he wrote the unrivalled 'History of the Russian Revolution'. He also produced 'The Permanent Revolution', a restatement of the theory which Stalin's propagandists held to be the original sin of Trotskyism, and 'The Stalin School of Falsification', in which he published important documents suppressed in the Soviet Union.

The second major task was to maintain and develop contacts with Left Oppositionists inside the USSR. The first issue of the 'Bulletin Oppozitisii' (Bulletin of the Opposition) was printed in Paris in July 1929. This little periodical helped to hold the Trotskyists together at a time when many leading opponents of Stalin were capitulating.

Thirdly, Trotsky threw himself into the work of building an International Left Opposition. Throughout the world there were small groups of anti-Stalinists, some of whom declared allegiance to Trotsky while others traced their existence to the Zinoviev Opposition, the Right Opposition (Bukharin's followers) and a variety of other splits in the Communist movement. Even among Trotskyists there were sometimes as many as four competing groups in single country.

Above: The London 'Evening Standard' reproduces 'Pravda's' virulent reaction to an article written by Trotsky for the 'Daily Express', February 1929.
When he arrived in Turkey, Trotsky was penniless save for a 'grant' of $1,500 from Stalin 'to enable him to settle abroad'. Trotsky sold a series of articles to the 'Express' and the New York 'Times' to raise money, but also to refute Stalin's story that he had left the USSR of his own free will. 'Pravda' declared that 'Mister Trotsky' had sold out to the imperialist press barons.
Above right: The Soviet cartoonist Victor Deni portrays Trotsky as a hireling, pen dripping with blood, for the cover of a pamphlet entitled 'No time even to spit on him', 1930.
Opposite page: Trotsky proudly displays a snoek which he has caught.

In the summer of 1929 Alfred Rosmer travelled to Belgium and Germany to meet Trotskyists there, while contact was made with groups in Italy, Holland, the United States and elsewhere. Trotsky conducted a vast correspondence with these groups, seeking to clarify their politics and to persuade them to unite where their differences did not justify separate organizations. Most important was France, where it was hoped to establish an international secretariat. The Trotskyists there were split into two main groups led by Pierre Naville and Raymond Molinier. Their factional squabbling, which surpassed even the intrigues of the pre-war Russian émigrés, infuriated and exasperated Trotsky, but he was obliged to intervene patiently and firmly almost every day.

Slowly the International Left Opposition began to take shape. Sections were established in thirty countries. They were mostly small: aside from the Russian section, only the Greek and Spanish counted more than 1,000 members. Almost everywhere, however, they could rely on a core of experienced militants, former leaders of the Communist Parties. The purpose of these sections was not to build new pareties, but to attempt to win the Communist Parties away from Stalin and back towards revolutionary internationalism. The International Left Opposition considered itself a faction of the Communist International even though its members had been expelled. 'We are for a united party', Trotsky wrote, referring to political conditions in the Soviet Union, 'so long as power has not passed into the hands of the bourgeoisie, i.e. so long as the Opposition can — given the right circumstances — fulfil its tasks by means of reform. A second party would shift the problem to the level of civil war.'

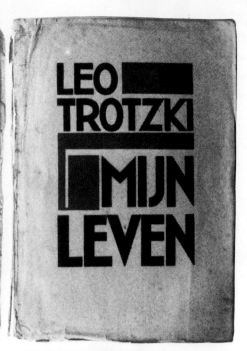

LES ÉDITIONS RIEDER

MITT LIV

NATUR och KULTUR

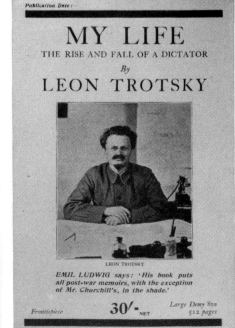

Above and left: 'My Life' in seven languages. Trotsky wrote this 'attempt at an autobiography' during 1928 and 1929. As literature it has been compared with Tolstoy and Gorky; as a twentieth-century history it is perhaps second only to Trotsky's own 'History of the Russian Revolution'. But first and foremost it was a political weapon in the hands of the International Left Opposition, refuting the accumulated lies of the Stalinist propaganda machine and educating a new generation of militants.

Far left: Alfred and Marguerite Rosmer, faithful friends of Trotsky's since the world war, arrived in Prinkipo from Paris in May 1929. They acted as Trotsky's literary agents and played a major role in bringing him into contact with his supporters in Europe, but they stood aside from the Naville and Molinier factions in France.

Opposite page: Pierre Naville, the lawyer Gerard Rosenthal and Denise Naville visiting Trotsky in the summer of 1930.

Top: Trotsky in his boat with a Greek fisherman, Kharalambos, who was almost illiterate but 'could read like an artist the beautiful book of Marmara'.

Above: The house in Hamladji Street, Prinkipo, where Trotsky lived from mid-January 1932 to July 1933. His first house on the island was damaged by fire in 1931, and his collection of photographs from the revolution was destroyed.

Above: Trotsky's cook displays an eel he has caught. She had a thankless job, for a secretary relates: 'I never heard him make a remark about the food.'

Top: Trotsky in his study at the villa Izzet Pasha, early 1931, before the accidental fire which forced the household to move. He is reading the newspaper of the Communist League of America, as the US Trotskyists were then known. They were the first group of the Left Opposition to establish a weekly newspaper.
Above, left to right: Jan Frankel, Lyova, Natalya, Jiri Kopp, and Trotsky. Frankel and Kopp were Czechoslovak militants who came to Prinkipo in 1930. Kopp soon returned, but Frankel remained one of Trotsky's closest aides.

Lyova was his father's closest political collaborator, and adored him almost to the point of personal identification. Trotsky would sometimes become impatient of his devotion, declaring that he longed for his son to show greater independence; yet if Lyova did so, he would become alarmed and upset.

The pressures of isolation heightened the tension between father and son. Trotsky had a tendency to take out on his family the frustration which he was careful to conceal from strangers, and Lyova suffered more than anyone. He was accused of 'sloth and sloppiness', 'letting down' his father and allowing the administrative work to slide into disorder. These unjust reproaches were naturally very upsetting to Lyova. At one stage relations became so unbearable that he even planned to return to the USSR.

Sadness was mingled with relief, therefore, when it was decided that Lyova and Jeanne Martin des Pallières (Raymond Molinier's wife, but now Lyova's lover) should move to Berlin. The German section needed strengthening, and it had been decided to transfer the international secretariat and production of the 'Bulletin Oppozitsii' to the German capital. They left on 1 March 1931.

219

Above: A studio photograph of Natalya soon after arrival in Turkey, 1929.
Left: Trotsky, Natalya and Lyova by the Sea of Marmara in 1930.

On 8 January 1931, a little while before Lyova's departure for Berlin, Trotsky's surviving daughter from his first marriage, Zina, arrived in Prinkipo with her five-year-old son Sieva. Her husband Platon had been deported to Siberia; she was suffering from tuberculosis; and she was increasingly fearful for herself and her children. She had to leave her six-year-old daughter in Leningrad.

She was physically as well as emotionally similar to her father. Her feelings towards him were of passionate attachment, pride and joy at the prospect of sharing his life and work. But she had seen little of him since early childhood, and beneath the adoration she nursed a deep scar. She continually doubted his love for her, and could never forget that he had abandoned her in Siberia twenty-nine years before. She was violently jealous of her half-brother Lyova, and resented Natalya. There were quarrels, and she succumbed to mental illness. Against her will Trotsky sent her to Berlin for psychoanalysis on 22 October, less than **220** nine months after her arrival.

She left Sieva with his grandparents, intending to rejoin him after completing her treatment. But in February 1932 Stalin deprived Trotsky, and hence his descendants, of Soviet citizenship. Zina, stateless, could no longer return to her son in Turkey.

When the boy had first arrived in Prinkipo Trotsky had been delighted with him and had revelled in the role of grandfather. But in time he came to resent Sieva's presence as a distraction and grew impatient to send him to his mother in Germany.

Above: Trotsky, Natalya and Abraham Sobolevicius, alias Adolf Senin, on a boating trip. Senin and his brother Ruvin, alias Roman Well, had joined the German Trotskyists in 1929 and had soon risen to positions of responsibility in the German group and the International Secretariat. In August 1931 they visited Trotsky in Turkey. Years later, when it was discovered that Senin and Well were GPU agents, Natalya defaced this picture and wrote 'Provocateur'. It is probable that other apparently trustworthy visitors to Prinkipo, such as the Lithuanian Jakob Frank who acted for five months as Trotsky's secretary, were Stalinist agents.
Left: A portrait photograph of Zina.
Opposite page: L.D. and Zina pose at Prinkipo with Senin (left) and Well.

During the course of 1928 and 1929 Stalinist domestic and foreign policy had swung dramatically from right to ultra-left. At home Stalin was now demanding the 'liquidation of the kulaks as a class' and the forcible collectivization of the peasants' land and means of subsistence. In January 1930 he was boasting that 50 per cent of farmsteads (about 13 million) had been collectivized in the previous four months. Civil war broke out in the countryside right across the Soviet Union; at the end of it unknown millions had been driven from their homes into Siberia and the Arctic Circle, or to their deaths, and agricultural production had declined catastrophically. Industrial output, meanwhile, was supposed to grow at a rate of 30, 40, 50 per cent a year. The workers, disorganized

and demoralized, faced starvation.

A parallel lurch to the left occurred in Comintern policy. It was announced that the post-war world had entered its Third Period: the first period of capitalist crisis and revolutionary advance (1917–24), and the second period of capitalist restoration (to 1928) had, quite inexplicably, given way to the third and final period — of capitalist collapse and worldwide proletarian victory. It was also discovered that the Socialist Parties were 'social fascist' and a greater danger to the working class than the fascists themselves.

Events in Germany soon put these 'theories' to the test. In March 1930 the government coalition of SPD (Socialist Party) and DVP (People's Party) had collapsed in the face of a deepening recession. For several months President Hindenburg ruled by decree until forced to call elections in

September. The SPD lost half a million votes, polling 8.6 million altogether (24.5 per cent); the KPD (Communists) increased their vote from 3.25 million to 4.6 million (13 per cent); but Hitler's Nazis leapt from 800,000 votes to 6.4 million, making them the country's second-largest party. The Brownshirts, now numbering 100,000, stepped up their attacks on Jews and workers.

The SPD reacted by blaming the Communists' extremism for Hitler's popularity, and they called on the police to restore 'law and order'; although there was a large Socialist defence force, it was hardly used.

The KPD proclaimed that the Nazis were no real threat, and they went as far as making alliances with them against the SPD. They split from the ADGB (General German Trade Union Federation), which was led by the Socialists, and formed their own 'red

union', the RGO (Revolutionary Trade Union Opposition). At the end of 1930 the ADGB had almost 5 million members, the RGO fewer than 150,000. Undeterred, the KPD leaders declared that even if Hitler came to power he would soon fail through incompetence, and 'after Hitler, it will be our turn'.

Trotsky tried desperately to warn the German working class of the dangers ahead and to reorientate the Communist Party. On 26 September 1930 he wrote: 'The gigantic growth of National Socialism is an expression of two factors: a deep social crisis, throwing the petty-bourgeois masses off balance, and the lack of a revolutionary party that would today be regarded by the popular masses as the acknowledged revolutionary leader. If the Communist Party

is the party of revolutionary hope, then fascism, as a mass movement, is the party of counter-revolutionary despair.'

The success of Hitler's Nazis, Trotsky explained, was a result of the blundering and sectarian policies of the Communist Party itself. The Nazis could only be stopped if the majority of the working class — and that meant the followers of the SPD — were won to revolutionary politics; then the petty-bourgeoisie would be drawn behind the workers, rather than the other way round. Naturally, Trotsky said, 'at the crucial moment the leaders of the Social Democracy will prefer the triumph of fascism to the revolutionary dictatorship of the proletariat. But precisely the approach of such a choice creates exceptional difficulties for the Social Democratic leaders among their own workers. The policy of a united front of the

Above: Hitler. The leaders of the German Communist Party declared that he was a lesser evil than the Social Democrats.

workers against fascism flows from this whole situation. It opens up tremendous possibilities for the Communist Party. A condition for success, however, is the rejection of the theory and practice of "social fascism", the harm of which becomes a positive menace.' With increasing desperation Trotsky hammered home these lessons over and over again during the next two and a half years. But his followers in Germany were a tiny minority; his advice was ignored.

פֿאַרװאָס סטאַלין נעמט
אַװעק מײַן בירגער רעכט

פֿון

לעאָן טראָצקי

אַן אָפּרוף בריװ צום פּרעזידיום פֿון צענטראַל
אױספֿיר קאָמיטעט פֿון סאָװעטן פֿאַרבאַנד

פּרײַז 5 סענט.

קאָמוניסטישע ליג פֿון אַמעריקע (אָפּאָזיציע)
84 East 10th Str New York, N. Y.

Above: 'Why Stalin Has Deprived Me
of Soviet Citizenship' by Leon Trotsky,
a Yiddish-language pamphlet published by the
Communist League of America in 1932.
Opposite page: 'The Only Road' (14 September 1932) —
one of many attempts by Trotsky to win
the German Communists to a policy of uniting
with the Socialists against Hitler.

20 Pfg.

Der einzige Weg

KPD

SPD

L. TROTZKI

In the autumn of 1932 Danish Social Democratic students invited Trotsky to deliver a lecture in Copenhagen. He accepted, and to his surprise he was granted a temporary visa. Armed with Turkish passports, Trotsky and Natalya, accompanied by three guards, left Prinkipo on 14 November and were rushed across Europe as though they carried the plague. Meanwhile Sieva was taken to Paris by Jean van Heijenoort, a young Frenchman who acted as Trotsky's secretary, and was put on the train for Berlin to rejoin his mother.

In Copenhagen Trotsky delivered a lecture in German to an audience of 2,000. He also recorded a broadcast in English for CBS radio, and a short propaganda film. He had other objectives: he renewed his efforts to find asylum in Europe — in vain; and he held a meeting with Oppositionists from France, Belgium, Italy, Holland, Britain, the United States and Germany.

The Stalinists tried to embarrass Trotsky by asserting that he was holding a 'secret conference', in violation of his visa conditions. Naturally, he was obliged to deny that a conference had taken place, but the 'consultations' were useful. He learned at first hand how several sections of the International Left Opposition were developing. (The information he gleaned was not always accurate, however. He was given the impression that the German section was showing good progress; in fact, led by the Stalinist agents Senin and Well, it was making little headway at a time of acute political crisis.)

The most common political problem facing the Left Opposition was how to conduct political work, for example in the trade unions, without turning their backs on the Communist Parties. Trotsky argued: 'The inclination of certain comrades (as in France) to interpret the role of the faction in such a sense that the Opposition must not take a single step outside of party limits is completely false ... It would be ridiculous to behave as if we belonged, in fact, to the official organizations of the Comintern ... We must turn to the workers where they are, we must go to the youth, teach them the ABC of communism, build cells in factories and trade unions. But this work must be carried on in such a manner that ordinary Communists can see that for us it is a question not of building a new party, but of reviving the Communist International.'

This nuanced political approach was not to the liking of all sections of the Opposition.

The Spanish group, led by Andrés Nin, declined to make the trip to Copenhagen. Trotsky was scathing: 'Perhaps the peculiar conditions in Spain justify the tactics of the Spanish Opposition, i.e. the course, in effect, towards a second party? Let us assume this is so. Why then don't the Spanish comrades attempt to explain these conditions to us and enrich us with their experience? Surely they do not believe that Spanish conditions cannot be understood outside of the borders of Spain? For in the latter case we would have to ask, "Why do we have an international organization at all?" ' Within two years Nin would answer this question by taking the majority of Spanish Oppositionists out of the Trotskyist movement and forming the semi-revolutionary POUM (Workers' Party of Marxist Unification) with supporters of the Bukharin-inspired Right Opposition.

Simultaneous pressure from the Stalinists and the Danish Royal Family (relatives of the Russian Tsars) resulted in the refusal of the Danish government to grant Trotsky even a few days' extension of his visa, and so he was forced to return in surly mood to Prinkipo. He was back by 11 December, as far as ever from the centre of political events.

Trotsky speaking in Copenhagen, 27 November 1932. This was Robert Capa's first published photograph.

**Above and left: During the Copenhagen meeting.
Bottom left: While he was in Denmark
Trotsky made a broadcast, in English, for CBS.**

233

On 5 January 1933 a cable arrived from Lyova in Berlin telling his parents that Zina had committed suicide — just a few days after Sieva had rejoined her. Before she died she had written Trotsky an incoherent letter full of reproaches, and to her mother in Leningrad: 'It is sad that I can no longer return to Papa. You know how I have adored and worshipped him from my earliest days. And now we are in utter discord. This has been at the bottom of my illness.' She had been deeply wounded when she learned that her father

had been sending to her psychoanalyst the letters she had written to him. Doubtless Trotsky believed he was helping to cure her, but to Zina this must have seemed a final act of betrayal.

Alexandra had now lost both of her children, and she wrote to Trotsky of Zina: 'You, her father, you could have saved her.' Why had he insisted on her undergoing psychiatric treatment? 'She was closed in herself — as we both are — and one should not have pressed her to talk about things she did not want to talk about.' Speaking of her grandchildren, she said, 'I do not believe in

life any longer. I do not believe that they will grow up. All the time I am expecting some new disaster.' Trotsky and Natalya shut themselves in their room for several days; when he emerged his hair was almost white.

**Above: Zina at Moda near Kodikoy, Turkey, in 1931, two years before her suicide.
Opposite page: This photograph of Zina was found in the archives of the Central Intelligence Agency in Washington, DC.**

Political tragedy followed hard on the heels of personal bereavement. On 30 January 1933 Hitler became Chancellor of the German Reich, and proceeded to destroy the trade unions and all oppositional parties. KPD members were rounded up and taken to concentration camps.

By early March it had become obvious to Trotsky that the German working class had suffered a definitive and catastrophic defeat. On the 14th he wrote 'The Tragedy of the German Proletariat':

'The criminal role of the Social Democracy requires no commentary: the Comintern was created fourteen years ago precisely in order to snatch the proletariat from the demoralizing influence of Social Democracy. If it has not succeeded up to now, if the German proletariat found itself impotent, disarmed and paralysed at the moment of its greatest historic test, the direct and immediate blame falls upon the leadership of the post-Leninist Comintern.' Recalling the capitulation of the socialist parties to nationalism in August 1914, he continued:

'It must be said clearly, plainly, openly: Stalinism in Germany has had its 4 August. Henceforth the advanced workers will only speak of the period of the domination of the Stalinist bureaucracy with a burning sense of shame, with words of hatred and curses. The official German Communist Party is doomed. From now on it will only decompose, crumble and melt into the void ... Under the terrible blows of the enemy, the advanced German workers will have to build up a new party.'

Even now Trotsky hesitated to turn his back on the entire Comintern; he still hoped that the shock of the German events would stir opposition in other Communist Parties. But by 15 July he was obliged to write:

'The Moscow leadership has not only proclaimed as infallible the policy which guaranteed victory to Hitler, but has also prohibited all discussion of what occurred. And this shameful interdiction has not been violated, nor overthrown. No national congresses; no discussions at party meetings; no discussion in the press! An organization which is not roused by the thunder of fascism and which submits docilely to such outrageous acts of the bureaucracy demonstrates thereby that it is dead and that nothing can ever revive it.'

The decision to write off the Comintern was taken with extreme reluctance not merely because Trotsky himself had been, with Lenin, its chief architect. The Fourth International and its national parties would have to be built almost from scratch under the most unfavourable conditions, in the shadow of the greatest defeat ever suffered by the working-class movement. And there was very little time, for a new world war was on the horizon.

An opportunity to win support for the building of a new international came in the summer, when the British Independent Labour Party called a conference open to all organizations outside the Second and Third Internationals to discuss political perspectives following the Nazi victory. The Trotskyists, now calling themselves the International Communist League, persuaded three other organizations to sign a declaration proclaiming the need for a new international and committing themselves to prepare for it: the German SAP — a group led by Right Oppositionists — and two Dutch organizations. The SAP soon changed its mind, but the Dutch groups fused to form the Revolutionary Socialist Workers Party, a sizeable formation which became for a time the section of the Trotskyist movement in Holland.

Below: A copy of the 'Bulletin Oppozitsii', November 1932, reduced to the size shown here for smuggling into the USSR.
Opposite page: Trotsky with aides, May 1933. Arne Swabeck (an American) and Pierre Frank (a Frenchman) are standing; squatting are Jean van Heijenoort (French) and Rudolf Klement (German).

234

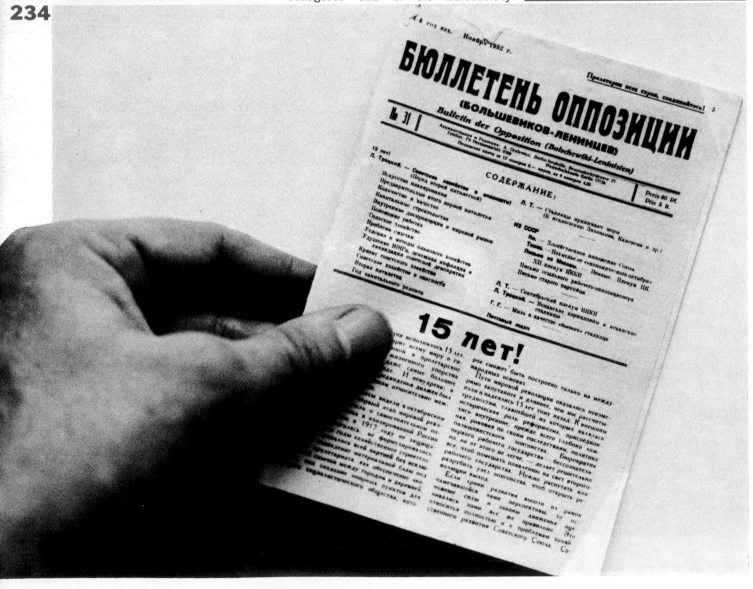

Lyova escaped from Germany at the end of March 1933, and set to work re-establishing the international headquarters in Paris. In July Trotsky received some good news: the efforts of his friends had borne fruit, and he would be permitted to move to France. At last he could escape his Turkish backwater!

By dint of some careful ruses Trotsky and his party managed to reach the small town of St Palais, near Royan, on 25 July without the GPU or newspaper reporters learning of their whereabouts. Trotsky was ill with lumbago and fever throughout most of the two months that they stayed there, and he seldom ventured far from the house. But he received a stream of visitors, most of whom came to discuss the idea of a new international: Jenny Lee from the British Independent Labour Party (and wife of Aneurin Bevan); Henricus Sneevliet from Holland, former Communist leader and Comintern emissary in Indonesia; and leaders of Belgian, German and Italian groups. Another visitor was the writer André Malraux, who published an account of their discussions on art and revolution and other topics.

From St Palais Trotsky and Natalya moved to a hotel in the Pyrenees. They made several short excursions, including a visit to Lourdes, of which he later wrote: 'A shop for miracles, a business office for trafficking in grace ... Indeed, the thinking of mankind is

bogged down in its own excrement.' Meanwhile Raymond Molinier had found them a house at Barbizon, 30 miles south-east of Paris. The stay in St Palais had caused the French authorities so little trouble that they consented to the move.

Left: Jean van Heijenoort leaving the French Consulate in Istanbul with visas under his arm for Trotsky and Natalya, 12 July 1933. With him is Max Shachtman. Above: Trotsky exercising the guard dogs Benno and Stella outside the villa Sea Spray, St Palais, August – September 1933.

From Barbizon Trotsky made regular, albeit surreptitious, visits to Paris to confer with the international secretariat and the leaders of the French section. Political conditions were favourable to the Trotskyists: their meetings calling for a united front of Communist and Socialist Parties against fascism were well-attended, and their membership grew. Right-wingers attacked the Chamber of Deputies on 6 February 1934, intending to bring down the government; the left organized a huge counter-demonstration on the 12th. French politics were becoming increasingly polarized.

Unfortunately the activities of the unusual household at Barbizon attracted the attention of the local police (who had not

been informed of Trotsky's presence). On 12 April they stopped Rudolf Klement on the pretext that his motorbike headlight was out of order, and arrested him. He was carrying political correspondence. In no time lurid stories were making headlines in the press. The government, under pressure from all sides, announced Trotsky's expulsion. Since no country would take him, the order was not immediately enforced, but he and Natalya had to leave Barbizon in a hurry. For weeks they wandered across France; eventually a haven was found in the home of a sympathetic schoolteacher in Domène, near Grenoble. They settled there in mid-July.

Right: St Palais, August 1933. With Trotsky
are Rudolf Klement, Yvan Craipeau
(a young French Trotskyist), Jeanne Martin
des Pallières (Lyova's lover), Sara Jacobs
(an American who knew Russian) and,
seated, Jean van Heijenoort.
Below left: The villa Ker Monique at
Barbizon where Trotsky stayed between
November 1933 and April 1934.
Below centre: A police report on Trotsky's
departure from Barbizon, mistakenly
stating that Natalya had remained behind
at the villa.
Below right: When Trotsky's whereabouts
were discovered in April 1934, newspaper
reporters — and busloads of sightseers —
descended on Barbizon. For several days
after he had left, van Heijenoort fooled
them into believing Trotsky was still inside:
he had discovered that they were bugging
the telephone, and 'I would simply give
fictitious details in a confidential manner
over the telephone.' Here he is chatting
with reporters.
Opposite page: Christian Rakovsky,
Siberia, 1932. This photograph was
smuggled out to Trotsky, who for two years
kept it beside his bed.

A little while before they left Barbizon, news came from the Soviet Union that Christian Rakovsky had capitulated to Stalin. Trotsky's own contacts with Oppositionists in the USSR had been completely stifled even while he was living on Prinkipo; but this announcement came as a terrible shock. Rakovsky had been a friend — perhaps Trotsky's closest personal friend — and unswerving political ally since the Balkan War days of 1912.

In 'My Life' Trotsky had written: 'Ch. G. Rakovsky is, internationally, one of the best-known figures in the European Socialist movement. A Bulgarian by birth, Rakovsky comes from the town of Kotel, in the very heart of Bulgaria, but he is a Rumanian subject by dint of the Balkan map, a French physician by education, a Russian by connections, by sympathies and by literary work. He speaks all the Balkan and four European languages; he has at various times played an active part in the inner workings of four socialist parties — the Bulgarian, the Russian, French and Rumanian — to become eventually one of the leaders of the

Soviet Federation, a founder of the Communist International, President of the Ukrainian Soviet of People's Commissars, and the diplomatic Soviet representative in England and France — only to share finally in the fate of all the Left Opposition. Rakovsky's personal traits, his broad international outlook, his profound nobility of character, have made him particularly odious to Stalin, who personifies the exact opposite of these qualities.'

After Trotsky's expulsion, Rakovsky became the leader of the Opposition in the Soviet Union. Where others such as Radek and Preobrazhensky (not to mention Zinoviev and Kamenev) compromised their principles with Stalin, Rakovsky stood firm. But Stalin had him isolated, and he was also very ill. In 1932 he tried to escape, but was captured and wounded. In February 1934, apparently influenced by the rise of Hitler, he gave up the struggle against Stalin. He was executed in 1941.

Immediately upon hearing the news of Rakovsky's capitulation, Trotsky made the official announcement: 'We register the purely formal declaration of the old warrior, who by his whole life demonstrated his unshakeable

devotion to the revolutionary cause; we register it with sadness, and pass on to the order of the day.' But his diary tells a more personal story: 'Rakovsky was virtually my last contact with the old revolutionary generation. After his capitulation there is nobody left. Even though my correspondence with Rakovsky stopped, for reasons of censorship, at the time of my deportation, nevertheless the image of Rakovsky has remained a symbolic link with my old comrades-in-arms. Now nobody remains. For a long time now I have not been able to satisfy my need to exchange ideas and discuss problems with someone else.'

The reference to an image of Rakovsky was quite literal. In 1932 a photograph of him was smuggled out from Siberia; Trotsky kept it by his bed. Van Heijenoort relates: 'One day in April 1934, after Rakovsky's capitulation to Stalin, I was burning worthless papers, such as translation drafts, in the garden of the Barbizon villa. Trotsky came to me, gave me Rakovsky's picture, and said: "Here, you can burn that too." ' Fortunately van Heijenoort disobeyed.

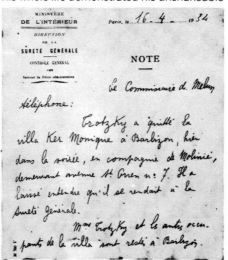

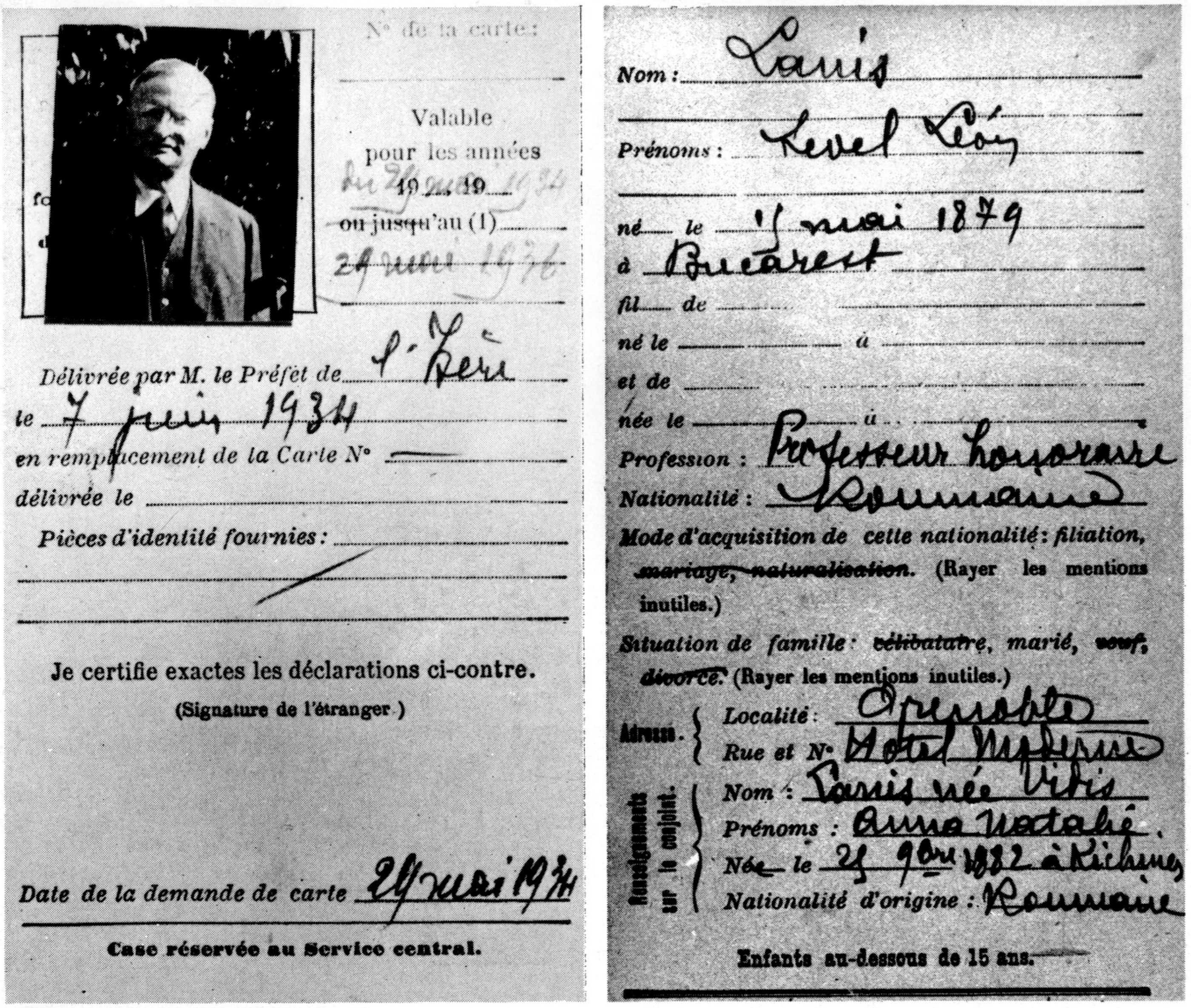

N° de la carte : _____

Valable
pour les années
19 __ 19 __
ou jusqu'au (1) _____

Délivrée par M. le Préfet de _____

le 7 juin 1934

en remplacement de la Carte N° _____

délivrée le _____

Pièces d'identité fournies : _____

Je certifie exactes les déclarations ci-contre.

(Signature de l'étranger.)

Date de la demande de carte _____

Case réservée au Service central.

Nom : *Lanis*

Prénoms : *Level Léon*

né le *1 mai 1879*

à *Bucarest*

fil__ de _____

né le _____ à _____

et de _____

née le _____ à _____

Profession : *Professeur honoraire*

Nationalité : *Roumaine*

Mode d'acquisition de cette nationalité : filiation, mariage, naturalisation. (Rayer les mentions inutiles.)

Situation de famille : célibataire, marié, veuf, divorcé. (Rayer les mentions inutiles.)

Adresse { Localité : *Grenoble*
{ Rue et N° : *Hôtel Moderne*

Renseignements sur le conjoint { Nom : *Lanis née Vitis*
{ Prénoms : *Anna Natalie*
{ Née le *24 9bre 1882 à Kichinev*
{ Nationalité d'origine : *Roumaine*

Enfants au-dessous de 15 ans.

240

Above: In June 1934 the French police consented to Trotsky's staying at Domène, near Grenoble. They kept him under close surveillance, and provided him with fake identity papers in the name of Level Léon Lanis (the surname belonged to Raymond Molinier's lover).
Opposite page: Before Domène, Trotsky, Natalya and van Heijenoort moved into a guest house in La Tronche, near Grenoble. It turned out to be a royalist stronghold. To avoid taking meals with the other residents, Trotsky and Natalya feigned a bereavement — hence the armband.

The political situation was now changing rapidly. In France the Communist Party was taking the first faltering steps towards an anti-fascist alliance with the SFIO (Socialists). Paradoxically, the fact that the Trotskyists' agitation for a united front was proving successful only made their own position more difficult: workers now flocked to join — or rejoin — the major parties.

On 4 July 1934 Trotsky wrote: 'It is necessary to go to the masses. It is necessary to find a place for oneself within the framework of the united front, i.e. within the framework of one of the two parties of which it is composed. In actual practice, that means within the framework of the SFIO.' Unlike the Stalinist party, the SFIO was a relatively loose federation; it had just sloughed off its own right wing; and it was openly calling on revolutionary-minded workers and groups to join it. It should be possible, Trotsky argued, to reach the rank and file of the SFIO with revolutionary arguments without making any sacrifice of political principle.

This tactic, known as 'entrism' and sometimes described as the 'united front from within', was not altogether new. In somewhat different circumstances Lenin had advised the British Communists to seek affiliation to the Labour Party; Trotsky even sought a parallel in Marx's entry into the German democratic party in 1848. More recently British Trotskyists had been urged to join the ILP in the hope of winning it to their politics, but they had split over the suggestion and the opportunity had been botched. The arguments Trotsky now advanced were applicable to most sections of the ICL; the 'French turn' was closely watched and hotly debated throughout the organization.

The internal life of the French section was scarcely any better now than it had been at the group's foundation. When the majority voted in favour of entry at a conference at the end of August, Pierre Naville and his followers refused to abide by the decision. The followers of Molinier proceeded to establish the GBL (Bolshevik-Leninist Group) as a faction of the SFIO in September. Naville subsequently also joined the SFIO, but refused to rejoin the GBL. Despite this idiocy, Trotskyist influence grew quite rapidly, especially among the youth wing of the SFIO.

Trotsky himself played a significant role in the life of the SFIO and its trade union affiliate in the Grenoble region — not in person, naturally, but through a young teacher named Bardin, for whom he wrote several important speeches. Trotsky was so careful to conceal his involvement that it was not fully appreciated, even by his own followers, until the mid-1960s.

Within a year of the GBL's entry into the SFIO, the Communist and Socialist leaderships had both moved far to the right, and were now joining the Radicals in the first formal Popular Front (cross-class alliance). The presence of revolutionaries became inconvenient to the SFIO leaders, and expulsions began. Trotsky demanded that his followers break from the reformist party, taking as many supporters with them as possible. But where there had been reluctance to join the SFIO, now there was resistance to the idea of leaving. The Trotskyists split again, in the process losing most of the benefits obtained from the entry.

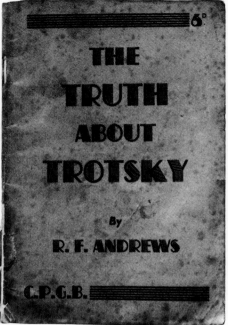

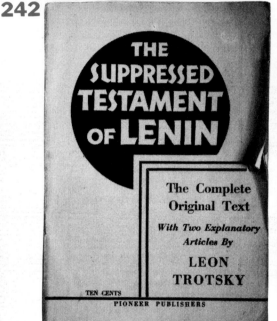

At the end of 1934 Trotsky was in Domène. He had just published 'Whither France?', an essay intended to orientate his supporters in the rapidly changing French political climate. On 1 December news came of the assassination of Sergei Kirov, Secretary of the Communist Party in Leningrad since Zinoviev's disgrace. At first the Soviet press and radio spoke of a White plot, but then, without explanation, described the assassin, one Nikolayev, as a follower of Zinoviev.

Nikolayev and fourteen other Young Com-

munists were executed, Zinoviev and Kamenev expelled from the Party (for the third time), arrested and held for trial. But the GPU seem to have bungled the affair. Attempts to associate Trotsky with the 'conspiracy' failed, and the two leading defendants were sentenced to ten and five years in prison — surprisingly lenient if one forgets that they were, of course, innocent.

Nevertheless the aftermath of the Kirov affair was extremely serious. Thousands of Trotskyists, Zinovievists — and Stalinists — were herded into concentration camps in the Soviet Union. Repression bore down more heavily on Trotsky's two sons-in-law, already deported since 1928; his first wife Alexandra, now over sixty, was expelled to Siberia; and his younger son Sergei disappeared, evidently arrested. Sergei was a lecturer at the Higher Technological Institute in Moscow, and completely non-political. In all the years since Trotsky and Natalya had been expelled from the Soviet Union he had written only to his mother, and had never so much as alluded to a political topic. Yet now Stalin had taken him hostage.

His parents were distraught. Natalya even

wrote an appeal for his release in the 'Bulletin Oppozitsii', but his fate was shrouded in silence. Trotsky now reached the conclusion that Stalin could not turn back from the path of terror, and would soon send the executioners after him. He wrote in his diary: 'There is now no one except me to carry out the mission of arming a new generation with a revolutionary method over the heads of the leaders of the Second and Third Internationals. And ... the worst vice is to be more than fifty-five years old! I need at least about five more years of uninterrupted work to ensure the succession,' that is, to establish the Fourth International on firm foundations.

His personal position in France was becoming increasingly dangerous. The Stalinist press wrote of 'Trotsky's hands covered with Kirov's blood'; Trotsky was the 'leader of world counter-revolution'. In May 1935 the French and Soviet governments formed an alliance; now bourgeois, Socialist and Stalinist parties were firmly wedded in the Popular Front. It was imperative to leave the country at the first opportunity.

In Norway the Labour Party won a general election in the spring of 1935. This party had been affiliated to the Third International in its early days; later it withdrew, but did not join the Second; and some of its leaders professed 'Trotskyist' sympathies. Trotsky applied for a visa, and after a delay of many weeks it was granted. Norwegian officials did their best to obstruct him, forcing him on 12 June to cable the Norwegian Prime Minister: 'The French government believes that I have deceived it, and demands that I leave France within 24 hours. I am sick and my wife is sick. Situation is desperate. I solicit immediate favourable decision.' To make matters worse, he was penniless and had to borrow the money for his and Natalya's fares.

On the 13th they were finally able to leave. They travelled first to Antwerp, where he held discussions with the leadership of the Belgian group, then they boarded the 'Paris', bound for Oslo. 'Nobody paid any attention to us,' Trotsky recorded in his diary. 'From that point of view the whole trip — unlike our previous migrations — was ideal ... N. and I travelled on émigré passports issued by the Turkish government; since Van (Heijenoort) and Frankel were with us, the officer in charge of tickets and passports defined our group in this way: "A Frenchman, a Czecho-slovak and two Turks."' They arrived on the 18th, and by the 23rd they were settled into the house of Konrad Knudsen, a journalist and Labour MP, 40 miles from the capital.

The Labour Party evidently enjoyed the glamour of acting as hosts to such a famous

revolutionary. The Minister of Justice, Trygve Lie, warned Trotsky that he was to refrain from political activity, and then proceeded to interview him for the party press on all the main issues of world politics. The conservatives, fascists and Stalinists organized protests inside and outside parliament, but they

caused him little inconvenience. For the first time in many years he lived openly and without guards. The main constraint on his activity was illness; in September he was admitted to hospital in Oslo.

These were times of stormy class struggle — mass sit-down strikes in France, armed

resistance to Franco in Spain. An international conference was arranged for August 1936, and Trotsky wrote the key political perspectives document ('The New Revolutionary Upsurge and the Tasks of the Fourth International'). The international movement had suffered several serious reverses in recent times, including the defection of the Greek section and most of the Spanish (Nin's followers); the Dutch would soon follow. Nevertheless Trotsky insistently urged that the conference then and there declare the foundation of the Fourth International; but the majority of what was scarcely a representative gathering declined, declaring themselves to be the more modest 'Movement for the Fourth International'.

Left: Aboard the 'Paris' en route from Antwerp to Oslo, June 1935.
Above: A picnic at Randesfund, 5 August 1936, on a trip to the fjords. Trotsky's host in Norway, the socialist journalist and member of parliament Konrad Knudsen, is wearing the white shirt. The same evening fascist followers of Quisling raided Knudsen's house in Wexhall (right).

The manuscript of 'The Revolution Betrayed' was completed by the beginning of August 1936. In this book, one of the outstanding works of Marxist theory, Trotsky attempted to analyse the contradictory nature of the state created by the revolution and to evaluate its present and future under Stalin. This task was all the more necessary in view of Stalin's recent announcement that socialism had 'completely triumphed' in the Soviet Union. The very purpose of revolutionary activity had to be stated anew.

Trotsky examined every aspect of the Stalinist reality: the economy, conditions of work, the growing inequalities in personal wealth, suppression of the rights won by women during the revolution, the suppression of artistic creativity, foreign policy, the nature of the ruling bureaucracy and the tasks of revolutionaries. He rejected as without content suggestions that the Soviet régime was 'state capitalist' and that the Stalinist bureaucracy was a 'new ruling class'. In many respects it closely resembled the fascist bureaucracy, but differed — crucially — in that its power derived from control of an economy in which the principal means of production were in the hands of the state. Its position was acutely contradictory, and its future as yet not determined. It could prepare the way for the restoration of capitalism, it could perhaps convert itself into a new ruling class possessed of the right to transmit ownership of the means of production from parent to child, or it could be swept away by a resurgent working class.

'Doctrinaires will doubtless not be satisfied with this hypothetical definition,' Trotsky added. 'They would like categorical formulae: yes — yes, and no — no ... There is nothing more dangerous, however, than to throw out of reality, for the sake of logical completeness, elements which today violate your scheme and tomorrow may wholly overturn it.' In any case, he concluded, 'the bureaucracy can be removed only by a revolutionary force ... The revolution which the bureaucracy is preparing against itself will not be social, like the October revolution of 1917. It is not a question this time of changing the economic foundations of society, of replacing certain forms of property with other forms ... The overthrow of the Bonapartist caste will, of course, have deep social consequences, but in itself will be confined within the limits of political revolution.'

On 4 August, immediately after finishing the Preface for 'The Revolution Betrayed', Trotsky left with his host Knudsen for a holiday in the fjords. In their absence followers of the fascist leader Major Quisling burgled the house, hoping to find incriminating material. The following morning Knudsen heard on the radio the announcement that Zinoviev, Kamenev and fourteen others would stand trial for treason, conspiracy and attempts to assassinate Stalin. Chief instigators of these crimes were Trotsky and Lyova, in collusion with the Gestapo. Trotsky was dumbfounded. 'Terrorism? Terrorism?' he kept repeating. 'Well, I can still understand this charge. But Gestapo? Did they say Gestapo? Are you sure of this?' The indictment included the claim that Trotsky was using Norway as a base for the despatch of terrorists to the Soviet Union.

Left: Trotsky in the Norwegian countryside, engaged in his favourite sport of shooting. Opposite page: 'Krokodil', August 1936, joins the campaign to brand Trotsky as a fascist.

№ 24 АВГУСТ — ИЗДАНИЕ ГАЗЕТЫ „ПРАВДА" — МОСКВА 1936

КРОКОДИЛ

Рис. К. Ротова

The nightmare summer of 1936.
Trotsky, 'ears glued to the wireless set', listens to Radio Moscow's
account of the trial of the 'Trotskyite-Zinovievite terrorists'.
Here is an extract from the 'final plea' of Mrachkovsky,
a worker-Bolshevik who had organized the insurrection in the Urals
in 1917: 'In 1923 I became a Trotskyite. I took a despicable path,
the path of deception of the Party ... Why did I take
the counter-revolutionary path? My connection with Trotsky —
that is what brought me to this ... The Party did all it could to tear
me away from counter-revolution. The Party helped
me and helped me a great deal. I depart as a traitor to my Party,
as a traitor who should be shot. All I ask is that I be believed
when I say that during the investigation I spat out all this vomit.'
Chief Prosecutor Vyshinsky concluded his oration:
'I demand that dogs gone mad should be shot — every one of them!'
Left: Waiting to give evidence in an Oslo court against
the fascist burglars of Konrad Knudsen's house, 28 August 1936.
With Trotsky is his Czechoslovakian secretary Erwin Wolf.

'The Case of the Trotskyite-Zinovievite Terrorist Centre' was heard in Moscow between 19 and 24 August 1936. Former leaders of the world revolutionary movement were paraded before the court, grovellingly confessing to the most fantastic crimes. Zinoviev's and Kamenev's confessions to the murder of Kirov were mere details.

It was imperative that Trotsky reply at once to the accusations levelled against him because, fantastic as they were, their constant repetition and elaboration had an effect. Many radicals of those times found it easier to believe the confessions than to grasp the enormity of what was happening in the Soviet Union. It was now that Justice Minister Lie found Trotsky's freedom to speak inconvenient. When, on 28 August,

Trotsky appeared in an Oslo court to testify in the case of Quisling's thieves, he was treated as though he were the defendant. Straight from the courtroom he was taken to the Ministry of Justice and asked to sign a document agreeing, among other things, to censorship of all communications to or from himself, Natalya and his secretaries. He refused. His secretaries were deported and he was interned.

It was left to Lyova in Paris to respond. He rose brilliantly to the occasion with 'The Red Book on the Moscow Trial'. Trotsky described it as 'a priceless gift ... the first crushing reply to the Kremlin falsifiers'. Yet the falsifiers were not crushed; they were already preparing for a second, and even more hallucinatory, trial. Meanwhile Oppositionists were being herded in tens of thousands into 'isolators' (concentration camps) all over the Soviet Union.

It was doubtless with relief that Lie could announce to Trotsky in mid-December that his friends' efforts had opened the doors of Mexico to him. He was given twenty-four hours to prepare himself; on the 19th he and Natalya were put aboard a petrol tanker, the 'Ruth', bound for Tampico.

Above and opposite page: Boris Efimov, the caricaturist, had flattered Trotsky while he was in power, but now he was prepared to deal out the most grotesque lies in the service of the Stalinist state, as this caricature labelled 'Terror' shows.

MEXICO 1937-1940

THE STRUGGLE FOR THE FUTURE

Trotsky at the age of fifty-seven, photographed at the time of his arrival in Mexico. 'I do not despair ... Three revolutions have made me patient.'

The journey to Mexico lasted twenty-one days, which Trotsky and Natalya were obliged to pass in the company of the ship's captain and a fascist Norwegian policeman.

It was a relief to escape the stifling hypocrisy of Socialist Norway; and the voyage allowed Trotsky to prepare his refutation of the confessions of Zinoviev and Kamenev. The sense of freedom was qualified, however, by anxiety at the unknown future awaiting them in Mexico.

The 'Ruth' drew into the great oil terminal of Tampico on a hot tropical morning, 9 January 1937. A government cutter came alongside, carrying federal officials, journalists — and friends: Frida Kahlo, artist and wife of the celebrated painter and muralist Diego Rivera; Max Shachtman, a leader of the Trotskyist movement in the US; and George Novack, secretary of the American Committee for the Defense of Leon Trotsky. The Mexican government — which still bore aloft the banner of popular revolution — provided a special train to carry the party to the capital. Then they travelled by car to the suburb of Coyoacán, where they were lodged in the beautiful Blue House in the Avenida Londres as guests of Frida and Diego.

Above: Trotsky has a haircut before landing in Mexico. Top: Disembarking at Tampico with Natalya. Above left: With Diego Rivera. Opposite page: Natalya poses — a little awkwardly — with Frida Kahlo.

2c

TRU

ABOUT THE MO

No. 1   NEW YO

TROTSKY
MOSCO

John Dewey Hea

Noted Publicists Hear Trotsky; Stalinists Fear To Face Issue

HE

A preliminary Commission of Inquiry headed by Dr. John Dewey, America's foremost liberal educator and philosopher, began this week in Mexico to take the testimony of Leon Trotsky as the first phase of the work of an international commission of inquiry into the Moscow tria

The demand for an impartial commission of i ed in this country and abroad by great labo

Published by
PIONEER PUBLISHERS
100 Fifth Ave., New York
Bundle orders $1 per 100.
Send checks or money
order with orders.

Editor: MAX SHACHTMAN

JTH

COW TRIALS

2K, N. Y.   401   APRIL, 1937,

BARES
W FRAUD

ds Mexico Inquiry

DOES NOT CONFESS!

ONLY TRUTH – CAN UNMASK FRAME - U P

These pages seek
truth about th
the most
h

The Committee for the Defense of
Leon Trotsky produced this broadsheet
in New York in April 1937.

259

Within a fortnight of their arrival, Moscow announced the trial of seventeen more leading Communists, including Karl Radek. Now Trotsky and Lyova were said to have entered into formal agreements with Hitler and the Mikado to destroy the Soviet Union. Sergei was charged with plotting the mass murder of workers by means of poison gas. Lie followed lie in hallucinatory parade; the only reality was the executioner's bullet.

It was imperative for Trotsky to make an effective response, not least in the hope of saving the lives of Stalin's prisoners. Despite gross intimidation from the 'Friends of the USSR', the American philosopher John Dewey had agreed to chair an independent commission of inquiry into the Moscow trials. His fellow members were well-known academics and journalists; only Alfred Rosmer was an associate of Trotsky's. The commission first met in March. A sub-committee travelled to Mexico in April to hear Trotsky testify and to cross-examine him. These hearings, held in the Blue House behind barricades of cemented brick and sandbags, lasted for a week. Trotsky concluded his evidence in the following way: 'The experience of my life, in which there has been no lack either of success or of failures, has not only not destroyed my faith in the clear, bright future of mankind, but, on the contrary, has given it an indestructible temper. This faith in reason, in truth, in human solidarity, which at the age of eighteen I took with me into the workers' quarters of the provincial Russian town of Nikolayev — this faith I have preserved fully and completely. It has become more mature, but not less ardent.' Dewey closed the hearing with the words: 'Anything I can say will be an anti-climax.'

The full commission continued its deliberations until September; it then issued a formal report, summed up in the last two sentences: 'We therefore find the Moscow Trials to be a frame-up. We therefore find Trotsky and Sedov not guilty.' But this small voice of reason was scarcely heard amid the din of more portentous events.

Top: Trotsky and Natalya prepare evidence for the Dewey Commission.
Left: During the Commission's hearings in Mexico City between 10 and 17 April 1937. From left to right are Jean van Heijenoort, Albert Goldman (Trotsky's US lawyer), Trotsky himself, Natalya, and the Czech Trotskyist Jan Frankel.

Trotsky enjoyed his new surroundings greatly, when he had the opportunity to notice them. He was fascinated by native Mexican art, and could have found no better tutor in the subject than Diego Rivera. The two men were utterly different in temperament — Diego flamboyant, noisy and demonstrative, Trotsky methodical, reserved, almost pedantic. Nevertheless they got on very well; Trotsky could even forgive Diego his political pretensions and undisciplined behaviour.

Frida treated Trotsky with a familiarity that would have been intolerable had he not found her captivating. Their relationship became unmistakably flirtatious. Natalya was uncomfortable with Frida from the beginning, affecting a warmth towards her which she did not feel. By late June she was suffering torments of jealousy, and the atmosphere became so tense that Jan Frankel ventured to broach the subject with Trotsky.

The couple decided to separate for a while, and Trotsky left on 7 July to stay at a hacienda some distance from Mexico City. He and Natalya exchanged a stream of letters, angry, hurt, contrite, tender. By the 27th he was back in Coyoacán, infatuated with Natalya all over again. After this Frida kept her distance; Diego knew, or seemed to know, nothing of the drama, and his behaviour towards Trotsky remained cordial.

**Top left: Diego Rivera has decorated a table with flowers in celebration of Trotsky's 58th birthday and the 20th anniversary of the October Revolution, 26 October 1937.
Top right: Trotsky at work in his office.
Above: Dictating an article with the help of Rita Yalokevna and Jean van Heijenoort.
Opposite page: On an excursion to Teotihuacán, 30 miles from Mexico City.**

Tragedy pressed in around them. Natalya wrote of that time: 'We listened to the radio, we opened the mail and the Moscow newspapers, and we felt that insanity, absurdity, outrage, fraud, and blood were flooding us from all sides here in Mexico as in Norway.' On 25 April 1937 Hitler's bombers obliterated Guernica. Communists and other leftists were being enlisted in many countries to join the International Brigades. They were not being sent to fight for socialism, however, but to preserve the Popular Front coalitions in Spain and, by extension, France. In June the central republican government outlawed the POUM and arrested its leaders.

In the Soviet Union the butchery continued. At the end of May it was the turn of the Red Army: Commander-in-Chief Tukhachevsky and most of his generals were charged with treason and executed. Altogether 25,000 officers were eliminated in an orgy of destruction for which the Soviet Union would pay an enormous price in the early years of the world war.

In July Ignace Reiss, leader of an important GPU ring in western Europe, broke with Stalin. Horrified at the endless purges, which now engulfed a large number of Stalin's own followers in the Politburo and other high offices, Reiss returned his Order of the Red Banner and declared his adherence to the Fourth International. He warned that Stalin had decided to liquidate opposition abroad as he was doing at home. Sure enough, Andrés Nin, leader of the POUM, was killed by GPU agents in August.

Reiss himself was found dead in Switzerland on 4 September. This example did not quite deter two other GPU men, Krivitsky and Barmin, from seeking contact with Trotsky. Krivitsky warned Lyova that there was an agent provocateur in the Paris centre, but he was unable to name the man.

Above: Ignace Reiss, a former GPU officer who defected to the Fourth International and was murdered on 4 September 1937. Right: Orphans of Stalin — Reiss's son Roman, Nin's daughters Nora and Vera, and Zina's son Sieva — photographed in Paris.

Lyova rejected his comrades' pressing advice to leave Paris and join his father in Mexico. He declared that Paris was too important a battle post. But the degradation and execution of so many men and women whom he had grown up to admire and love gradually wore him down. He began to suffer from bouts of depression and insomnia.

At the beginning of February 1938 he developed appendicitis. Ignoring the symptoms, he continued to work until the 8th. He spent that day in the company of his closest friend Mordka Zborowski, known in the movement as Etienne. In the evening Etienne called an ambulance from the Mirabeau Clinic. Lyova gave Jeanne Martin a note, which she was to open only if an 'accident' should happen to him; he insisted that none of the French comrades, whom he mistrusted, should know of his whereabouts; and in the company of Jeanne and Etienne he rode to the hospital. He underwent a successful operation that evening, and was recovering rapidly. Then he began to suffer severe pains and loss of consciousness. He died on the 16th, at the age of thirty-two.

The Mirabeau Clinic, frequented by Russian émigrés, was owned by Dr Boris Girmounski, who had formerly served the Cheka in the USSR. He had been permitted to emigrate with his family, and had bought the clinic for 6 million francs. After the war it was established that Etienne, too, had been a GPU agent since 1934. It seems that Stalin and his GPU chief, Henrikh Yagoda, had personally supervised his infiltration of the Trotskyist movement.

The news of Lyova's death reached Coyoacán when an American journalist rang the house on Avenida Londres around midday on the 16th. Trotsky was not there: three days earlier he had secretly moved to a house in Chapultepec, on the other side of Mexico City, because there were signs that the GPU were preparing an attack. His secretaries hid the afternoon papers from Natalya and kept her from the phone while van Heijenoort went to find Diego Rivera. Together they travelled to Chapultepec.

'As soon as we entered the room where Trotsky was, Rivera stepped forward and told him the news directly. Trotsky, his face hardening, asked "Does Natalya know?" To Rivera's negative answer he replied, "I shall tell her myself." We left at once. I drove, with Rivera at my side. Trotsky sat in the back, stiff and silent. Upon arriving in Coyoacán, he immediately shut himself up with Natalya in their room.' When they emerged eight days later, the old man had written:

'His mother — who was closer to him than any other person in the world — and I are living through these terrible hours recalling his image, feature by feature, unable to believe that he is no more and weeping because it is impossible not to believe. How can we accustom ourselves to the idea that upon this earth there no longer exists the warm, human entity bound to us by such indissoluble threads of common memories, mutual understanding and tender attachment. No one knew us and no one knows us, our strong and our weak sides, as he did. He was part of both of us, our young part. By hundreds of channels our thoughts and feel-

267

ings daily reached out to him in Paris. Together with our boy has died everything that still remained young within us.

'Goodbye, Leon, goodbye dear and incomparable friend. Your mother and I never thought, never expected that destiny would impose on us this terrible task of writing your obituary. We lived in the firm conviction that long after we were gone you would be the continuer of our common cause. But we were not able to protect you. Goodbye Leon! We bequeath your irreproachable memory to the younger generation of workers of the world. You will rightly live in the hearts of all those who work, suffer and struggle for a better world. Revolutionary youth of all countries! Accept from us the memory of our Leon, adopt him as your son — he is worthy of it — and let him henceforth participate invisibly in your battles, since destiny has denied him the happiness of participating in your final victory.'

Above: Lyova photographed with his father at St Palais in August 1933.
Opposite page: Mordka Zborowski, alias Etienne. Lyova considered him his closest friend; but after the war he confessed that he had been a GPU agent since 1934.

Leon Sedov (Lyova) was second only to his father in importance as an organizer of the international revolutionary movement. He died in a Paris clinic in February 1938, probably from poisoning.
Below: The US and Chinese editions of Trotsky's obituary to his fallen son and comrade-in-arms.

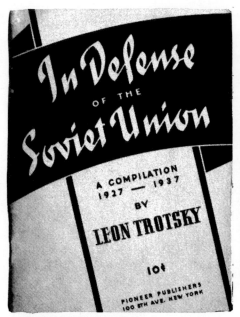

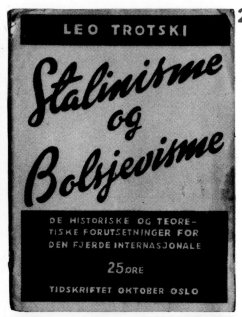

Alongside his analyses of Stalinism and the Soviet Union (top: pamphlets from the USA, Spain and Norway), Trotsky focused in his writings on political developments in Spain, where General Franco launched a fascist uprising in July 1936. The pamphlet on the left, above, was written in December 1937, while the one on the right had been published in Madrid in 1933. The article 'On the Spanish revolution and Stalinism' (above centre) appeared in the magazine of the French Trotskyists in March 1937. Far right: Jacques Doriot was a Communist mayor in Paris, sold to the electors as a 'man of destiny', who defected in 1936 to form a fascist party. The Stalinists tried to use him to smear Trotsky. In reply to the publication of slanders such as this Trotsky reissued in 1937 his exposé of the lie machine (right), first published in 1930. Opposite page: The original of all 'personality cults'. This photo shows a Communist meeting in Spain in 1938.

Lenin's Genera

STALIN, THE EXECUTIC

RYKOV
Shot

BUKHARIN
Shot

SVERDLOV
Dead

STALIN
Survivor

KOLLONTAI
Missing?

URITSKY
Dead

KRESTINSKY
Shot

SMILGA
Shot

LOMOV
?

SHOMYAN
Dead

BERZIN
?

MURANOV
Disappeared

NER, ALONE REMAINS

This grim gallery was compiled by the US Socialist Workers Party in March 1938.

ZINOVIEV
Shot

KAMENEV
Shot

TROTSKY
In Exile

LENIN
Dead

NOGIN
Dead

DZERZHINSKY
Dead

BUBNOV
Disappeared

SOKOLNIKOV
In Prison

ARTEM
Dead

STASSOVA
Disappeared

MILIUTIN
Missing

JOFFE
Suicide

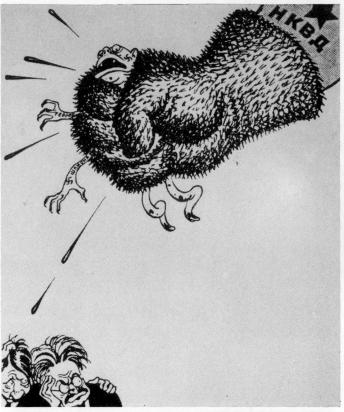

In Moscow the tumbrils were rolling again. In March Bukharin, Rykov and poor Rakovsky were thrust upon the stage in the third great show trial. Alongside them appeared Yagoda, puppet-master of the earlier trials, now confessing to having been a Trotskyite conspirator all along. His successor Yezhov in turn disappeared soon after this trial.

Meanwhile deep within the Polar Circle a far more terrible tragedy was being enacted. Already in 1935 there were an estimated five million men, women and children scattered in concentration camps across the Soviet Union. Throughout the next two years expulsions and arrests continued on a vast scale. In the autumn of 1937 convoy after convoy of Oppositionists travelled into the far north. There are three known accounts of what was then done. Here are extracts from one:

'Silent death carried off hundreds that first winter. Only the younger and stronger survived ... The bloody extermination of Communist Oppositionists and of people who had sympathized with them or had come into contact with them to one degree or another went on in 1937–38, not only at Adak but at all the campsites of the Vorkhuta-Pechora and Ukhta detention districts.

'The tragedy of the people who worked at the brick factory near Vorkhuta arouses a feeling of chill horror towards all the butchers who carried out their bloody work at that place. Under the pretext of transporting them to Obdorsk, the prisoners were led out into the tundra and shot down with machine guns or blown up by explosive charges planted in the snow beside the road ...

'The scarce, few witnesses who chanced by some miracle to survive from among

ФАТЕРЛЯНД

Opposite page: Caricatures on the theme 'Trotskyism equals fascism'.
The fist of the secret police (top right) is crushing 'terror' and 'spies';
the lightning spelling GPU (bottom right) is striking 'counter-revolutionary vermin'.
Above: Boris Efimov produced this disgusting caricature (of Trotsky, Rykov, Bukharin and others wallowing in a trough entitled 'Vaterland') to coincide with the third Moscow trial, 1938.

those who took part in the annihilation of the old Communists also told us that bathhouses at the brick factory had been rigged up as gas chambers for Oppositionists. Under the pretext of giving them sterilizing baths for hygienic purposes before they were to be shipped off, they herded people into these bathhouses, from which they never returned alive. The corpses were taken out into the tundra and burned.'

Along with their parents, all children aged twelve and above were massacred. No one knows how many were killed, but by the end of it scarcely anyone — whether Trotskyist, Zinovievist, Bukharinist or Stalinist — who had been a Bolshevik during the revolution or civil war was left alive.

It was apparently at Vorkhuta that Sergei died. In October 1936 he joined his father's co-thinkers in a hunger strike which lasted for 132 days and was not broken, and he was killed along with them in the winter of 1937. Trotsky never heard of his son's fate — though he and Natalya assumed the worst — nor of the extermination of his followers in the Soviet Opposition.

276

Above: Trotsky is filmed reading an exposé of the Moscow frame-ups, 26 February 1938. The book from which he is reading, by Max Shachtman, is shown below left. Below centre and right: A year earlier, on 16 February 1937, the American Trotskyists had organized a rally in the Hippodrome, New York, in refutation of Stalin's accusations. Trotsky was to address the meeting, in English and Russian, by telephone from the central exchange in Mexico City. Just as he was about to begin, the line went dead. In anticipation of such an 'accident', Max Shachtman in New York had been given a transcript of Trotsky's speech, and he read it instead. It ran, in part: 'I am ready to appear before a public and impartial Commission of Inquiry with documents, facts and testimonies . . . and to disclose the truth to the very end. I declare: If this Commission decides that I am guilty in the slightest degree of the crimes which Stalin imputes to me, I pledge in advance to place myself voluntarily in the hands of the executioners of the GPU . . . But if the Commission establishes . . . that the Moscow trials are a conscious and premeditated frame-up, I will not ask my accusers to place themselves voluntarily before a firing squad. No, eternal disgrace in the memory of human generations will be sufficient for them! Do the accusers in the Kremlin hear me? I throw my defiance in their faces, and I await their reply.' Mexican and US editions of the speech are reproduced below. Stalin's response was of a different order.

Opposite page: Sergei (Seryozha) with his brother Lyova's son, photographed in Moscow in 1934. They both perished at Stalin's hands.

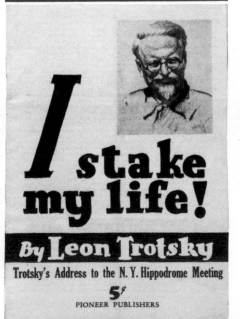

On an outing to Chapultepec Park, June 1938. From left to right: Diego Rivera, Frida Kahlo, Natalya, Reba Hansen, André Breton, Trotsky,

a Mexican Trotskyist, Jesús Casas (head of the police garrison guarding Trotsky's house), one of Rivera's drivers and Jean van Heijenoort.

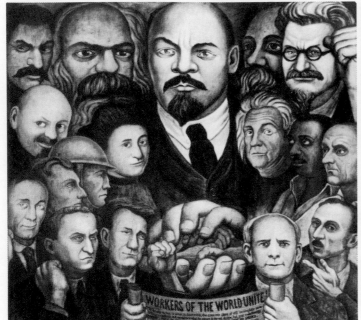

Top left: 'Proletarian Unity' by Diego Rivera, 1933. This was the central panel of a large mural entitled 'Portrait of America' painted at the New Workers' School, 14th Street, New York. Lenin dominates the scene, joining the hands of a black and a white worker, a farmer and a soldier. To his right are Engels and Trotsky, to his left Marx and, in the corner, Stalin. Below are Bukharin, Luxemburg (centre left) and Zetkin (centre right). In the left foreground are William Z. Foster, Stalinist Chairman of the American Communist Party; Jay Lovestone, leader of the Right Opposition; and James P. Cannon, foremost US Trotskyist. Rivera was here making a plea for Communist unity. In the right foreground are Charles E. Ruthenburg, General Secretary of the American CP until his death in 1927; and Bertram Wolfe, a Lovestoneite who collaborated with Rivera in producing a book based on the 'Portrait of America' murals.
Above left: The authors of the manifesto 'Towards a Free Revolutionary Art', Diego Rivera, André Breton and Trotsky, summer 1938.
Above right: Breton and Trotsky.
Opposite page: An outing, summer 1938. From left to right are Trotsky, Rivera, Natalya, Reba Hansen, Breton, Frida Kahlo and Jean van Heijenoort.

The French surrealist poet André Breton arrived in Mexico for a lecture tour in April 1938. He was an ardent admirer of Trotsky (though not of his French followers), and together with his wife visited Coyoacán at the beginning of May. Trotsky was keen to establish an organization of revolutionary artists and writers to counterbalance the 'cultural' activities of the Stalinists, and Breton's arrival provided him with an opportunity which he was determined not to miss.

Over the next two months Breton, Rivera and Trotsky held a number of discussions on the relationship between art and politics, out of which emerged a manifesto (mostly written by Trotsky though not signed by him) entitled 'Towards a Free Revolutionary Art'. It read in part:

'It goes without saying that we do not identify ourselves with the currently fashionable catchword: "Neither fascism nor communism!" — a shibboleth which suits the temperament of the philistine, conservative and frightened, clinging to the tattered remnants of the "democratic" past. True art, which is not content to play variations on ready-made models but rather insists on expressing the inner needs of man and of mankind in its time — true art is unable not to be revolutionary, not to aspire to a complete and radical reconstruction of society. This it must do, were it only to deliver intellectual creation from the chains which bind it, and to allow all mankind to raise itself to those heights which only isolated geniuses have achieved in the past. We recognize that only the social revolution can sweep clean the path for a new culture. If, however, we reject all solidarity with the bureaucracy now in control of the Soviet Union, it is precisely because, in our eyes, it represents, not communism, but its most treacherous and dangerous enemy.

'The totalitarian régime of the USSR, working through the so-called cultural organizations it controls in other countries, has spread over the entire world a deep twilight hostile to every sort of spiritual value. A twilight of filth and blood in which, disguised as intellectuals and artists, those men steep themselves who have made of servility a career, of lying for pay a custom, and of the palliation of crime a source of pleasure. The official art of Stalinism mirrors with a blatancy unexampled in history their efforts to put a good face on their mercenary profession.'

The statement of such revolutionary sentiments was as dangerous for an artist as it was for a politician. Trotsky was obliged to order his Mexican followers to protect Breton whenever he appeared in public.

Throughout the late spring and summer of 1938 the sections of the Trotskyist movement were engaged in political discussions in preparation for the founding congress of the Fourth International. This was to be the culmination of Trotsky's entire political work since 1933. By mid-April he had completed the draft of 'The Death Agony of Capitalism and the Tasks of the Fourth International'.

In this document, generally called the Transitional Programme, Trotsky tried to codify the experiences of the Bolsheviks, the Third International of Lenin's day, and the Left Opposition itself. In particular he drew together the theories of permanent revolution and the united front to produce a network of slogans or demands covering the major political issues of the contemporary world. The document begins:

'The world political situation as a whole is chiefly characterized by a historical crisis of the leadership of the proletariat ... All talk to the effect that historical conditions have not yet "ripened" for socialism is the product of ignorance or conscious deception. The objective prerequisites for the proletarian revolution have not only "ripened"; they have begun to get somewhat rotten. Without a socialist revolution, in the next historical period at that, a catastrophe threatens the whole culture of mankind. It is now the turn of the proletariat, i.e. chiefly of its revolutionary vanguard. The historical crisis is reduced to the crisis of the revolutionary leadership.'

The old social-democratic parties had generally divided their political programme into minimum and maximum demands — the former confined to reforms compatible with the continued existence of capitalism, and the latter to promises of a socialist paradise in some undefined future. The Bolsheviks had returned to the revolutionary tradition of Marx and Engels in advancing a system of demands 'which in their totality disintegrate the power of the bourgeoisie' (as the Communist International's Theses on Tactics put it). Trotsky in turn rescued and developed this revolutionary approach with the system of 'transitional demands'. He explained their significance as follows:

'The strategic task of the next period — a prerevolutionary period of agitation, propaganda and organization — consists in overcoming the contradiction between the maturity of the objective revolutionary conditions and the immaturity of the proletariat and its vanguard (the confusion and disappointment of the older generation, the inexperience of the younger generation). It is necessary to help the masses in the process of the daily struggle to find the bridge between the present demands and the socialist programme of the revolution. This bridge should include a system of transitional demands, stemming from today's conditions and from today's consciousness of wide layers of the working class and unalterably leading to one final conclusion: the conquest of power by the proletariat.' The Transitional Programme applied this method to the specific conditions of the advanced capitalist countries, colonial and semi-colonial countries, fascist countries, and the USSR.

Preparations were underway for the congress when Rudolf Klement, international secretary of the movement, disappeared. His horribly mutilated body was found in the Seine on 18 July.

Twenty-one delegates from eleven countries assembled at the home of Alfred Rosmer near Paris on 3 September. Trotsky was not, of course, present. Nor were Lyova, Klement or Erwin Wolf (Trotsky's secretary in Norway, murdered in Spain by the GPU): these three were elected honorary presidents. The Russian section — now effectively a small group of émigrés living in Paris — was represented by none other than Etienne. The congress adopted the Transitional Programme as its central programmatic document, and proclaimed the Fourth International. To this frail vessel Trotsky entrusted the traditions of revolutionary communism.

Left: 'La Lutte ouvrière' ('Workers' Fight'), newspaper of the French Trotskyist group, the POI (Internationalist Workers' Party), reports the disappearance of Rudolf Klement, 22 July 1938.
Bottom left: The bridge on the river Seine, Paris, where Klement's headless body was found on 18 July.
Below: The Transitional Programme, founding document of the Fourth International, in an edition published by a British Trotskyist group, the Workers International League.
Opposite page: Rudolf Klement.

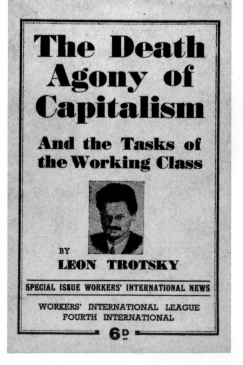

The Death Agony of Capitalism

And the Tasks of the Working Class

BY LEON TROTSKY

SPECIAL ISSUE WORKERS' INTERNATIONAL NEWS

WORKERS' INTERNATIONAL LEAGUE
FOURTH INTERNATIONAL

6D

The fortified house in the Avenida Viena, Coyoacán, to which Trotsky and his household moved on 5 May 1939.

One decision of the founding congress of the Fourth International had been to remove Rivera from membership of the Mexican section because of his disruptive influence; he was to work under the direct supervision of the International Secretariat.

Rivera was not one to accept such a decision with good grace. He spoke of resigning from political activity and devoting himself solely to painting. He quarrelled with Trotsky, and then became involved in political activity which Trotsky considered unprincipled. There was a public break. Thereafter it was

no longer possible to stay in the Blue House, and after a protracted hunt Trotsky's secretaries found him a new abode close by, in the Avenida Viena. They moved on 5 May.

The Rosmers, long awaited, arrived at the beginning of August. They brought with them Sieva, Zina's son. After his mother's suicide, Sieva had lived with Lyova and Jeanne Martin in Paris. When Lyova died, Trotsky invited Jeanne to join the Coyoacán household, but she refused. Nor would she let Sieva go. The issue went to court, and twice judgment was passed in favour of the grandparents. Jeanne still would not part with the little boy, and hid him. Eventually

the Rosmers found the poor child and — after a further attempt by Jeanne's friends to abduct him — took him to Mexico. Thus the bewildered twelve-year-old found himself in his grandfather's fortress.

Opposite page: Zina's son Sieva has arrived in Mexico in the custody of Marguerite and Alfred Rosmer after a bitter legal battle. Above: Alfred Rosmer accompanies L.D. on a hunt for cacti, which he collected. Below: A family picnic.

Daily life in the Avenida Viena,
illustrated in photographs assembled by
the US Trotskyist Farrell Dobbs.

The signing of the Hitler–Stalin pact on 23 August 1939, followed by the partition of Poland between the signatories, caused Communist Parties throughout the world to discover that the Nazi leader was not, after all, a threat to world peace. World War II began within a fortnight.

The outbreak of hostilities brought to a head a political crisis in the Trotskyist movement, especially in the US Socialist Workers Party. This group, led by James P. Cannon,

had practised the tactic of entrism with greater success than had the French, and had achieved a certain strength, notably among the Teamsters of Minneapolis-St Paul. It had also attracted a number of intellectuals, among them James Burnham, a professor of philosophy.

Trotsky, who had predicted the Stalin–Hitler pact, argued that the Soviet dictator's objective was to deflect the Nazi attack from the Soviet Union for as long as possible. This behaviour did not at all call into question the analysis of the Soviet Union as a 'workers' state' (by virtue of its socialized economic structure), albeit suffering from massive bureaucratic deformations. The Fourth International, he maintained, should continue to defend the workers' state against imperialist attack, but it should do so despite the bureaucracy — and indeed, against it.

Burnham had been voicing criticism of the 'workers' state' analysis for some time, though without drawing practical conclusions. But on the day that the Stalin–Hitler pact was announced, Max Shachtman, who had hitherto been proud of his 'orthodoxy', moved at a meeting of the SWP Political Committee 'That the next meeting of the Political Committee begin with a discussion of our estimate of the Stalin–Hitler pact as related to our evaluation of the Soviet state.'

Within weeks a ferocious factional fight was raging in the SWP, and it threatened to involve the whole International. Trotsky identified Burnham, Shachtman and their followers as a petty-bourgeois bloc buckling under the pressure of the anti-Soviet propaganda which engulfed the USA after the pact was signed. While his criticism of the opposition's political and theoretical pro-

nouncements was withering, he made strenuous efforts to prevent a split. He hoped in particular to hold on to Shachtman; privately and publicly (in the article 'From a scratch — to the danger of gangrene') he warned him where his alliance with Burnham would lead.

The breach could not be healed, however. Differences were expressed on an ever-widening range of issues: the validity of dialectical materialism (the philosophical basis of Marxism) and the internal régime of the party were soon challenged alongside the policy of the Fourth International in the war. Trotsky was inescapably confronted with a crisis which threatened to wreck the revolutionary movement.

The SWP convention called to decide the issues met during the first week of April 1940. The Trotsky–Cannon faction won a majority for a reaffirmation of established policy. The Burnham–Shachtman faction controlled the International Executive Committee of the International, however, so an emergency conference was convened in mid-May to debate the issues again and elect a new international leadership. By this time the minority had split from the SWP to form a rival party. (Within a month Burnham had resigned from his own group, declaring that he no longer considered himself a Marxist of any kind. He became a right-wing ideologue who years later denounced Nixon for being too soft on Moscow.)

The Fourth International was weakened numerically, but still intact. Its attitude towards the Second World War was generally that of the Leninists towards the First: Trotsky expected revolutionary upsurges to follow on the heels of the armed conflict; the task of the Fourth International was to encourage these and prepare to lead them. The bourgeois democracies, he thought, would not survive the war; nor would Stalin, as he wrote for the emergency conference: 'The epoch of great convulsions upon which mankind has entered will strike the Kremlin oligarchy with blow after blow, will break up its totalitarian apparatus, will raise the self-confidence of the working masses and thereby facilitate the formation of the Soviet section of the Fourth International. Events will work in our favour if we are capable of assisting them!' The difficulties of the post-war revolutionary movement, deprived of Trotsky's leadership, stemmed directly from the fact that the Stalinist régime proved to be more resilient than this.

'The attack came at dawn, about 4 a.m. I was fast asleep, having taken a sleeping drug after a hard day's work. Awakened by the rattle of gunfire but feeling very hazy, I first imagined that a national holiday was being celebrated with fireworks outside our walls. But the explosions were too close, right here within the room, next to me and overhead. The odour of gunpowder became more acrid, more penetrating ... My wife later told me that she helped me to the floor, pushing me into the space between the bed and the wall ... she had remained hovering over me, beside the wall, as if to shield me with her body ...

'As the shooting died down we heard our grandson in the neighbouring room cry out: "Grandfather!" The voice of the child in the darkness under the gunfire remains the most tragic recollection of that night. The boy — after the first shot had cut his bed diagonally, as evidenced by marks left on the door and wall — threw himself under the bed. One of the assailants, apparently in a panic, fired into the bed, the bullet passed through the mattress, struck our grandson in the big toe and imbedded itself in the floor. The assailants threw two incendiary bombs and left our grandson's bedroom. Crying "Grandfather!" he ran after them into the patio, leaving a trail of blood behind him and, under gunfire, rushed into the room of one of the guards.

'At the outcry of our grandson, my wife made her way into his already empty room. Inside, the floor, the door and a small cabinet were burning. "They have kidnapped Sieva," I said to her. This was the most painful moment of all. Shots continued to ring out but already away from our bedroom somewhere in the patio or immediately outside the walls. The terrorists were apparently covering their retreat. My wife hastened to smother the incendiary flames with a rug. For a week after she had to treat her burns.'

Trotsky remembered the night of 23–24 May in his article 'Stalin seeks my death'. He added: 'I can state that I live on this earth not in accordance with the rule but as an exception to the rule.' More than twenty men, heavily armed and dressed as policemen or soldiers, had overcome the Mexican sentries and Trotsky's guards and had systematically

Above: Trotsky with police after the Siqueiros raid, 24 May 1940.
Right: His bedroom riddled with bullets.
Top: Plaque erected at the Avenida Viena.
Left: David Alfaro Siqueiros (centre) under arrest, October 1940.

IN MEMORY OF ROBERT SHELDON HARTE 1915 – 1940. MURDERED BY STALIN.

set about the murder of the old man and his family. Fortunately their aim was poor, and a large bomb which they threw as they retreated failed to explode. None of the guards was killed or injured, but one — young Robert Sheldon Harte from the US Socialist Workers Party — was missing.

It was widely believed that Harte had been in league with the assailants, since it had been he who opened the gate to them, but Trotsky refused to believe it. The young man's body was eventually found on 25 June in the grounds of a farm rented by two painters, both Stalinists. Meanwhile the police caught several of the raiders, who testified that they had been led by another painter, David Alfaro Siqueiros, a leading member of the Communist Party. When arrested in October, Siqueiros admitted his role; released on bail, he left the country for some years; on his return all charges against him were dropped because the dossier relating to his crime had disappeared.

Natalya later described the atmosphere in the Avenida Viena after the attack: 'As I recounted the events of the GPU's night assault to friends ... I felt that I was relating this almost with joy. But those who listened heard me with alarm, they cast frightened glances towards the heads of the two beds, where the wall was dotted with bullet holes, and I would say to myself as if in justification: "But after all the enemies did suffer failure." The following days strengthened more and more in us the conviction that the failure suffered by our enemies on this occasion must be remedied by them; that the inspirer of this crime would not be deterred. And our joyous feeling of salvation was dampened by the prospect of a new visitation and the need to prepare for it.'

Robert Sheldon Harte (1915–1940).
The photo top left was taken
by police after his body had been
recovered from a lime pit.

Colonel Salazar, the chief of the Mexican Secret Service, at first believed that the Siqueiros attack had been staged by Trotsky as a publicity stunt. He was led to this conclusion by the behaviour of Trotsky himself, who passed the time before the police arrived working in his study. Salazar relates: 'I asked to see Trotsky, who soon arrived accompanied by his wife ... he was in pyjamas, over which he had slipped a dressing-gown. They greeted me with friendliness ... but they preserved a surprising calm. One might have thought that nothing had happened ... Trotsky smiled, with his eyes bright and clear behind his tortoiseshell glasses — eyes always keen and piercing.' The policeman, although he had himself been a soldier, could not understand the self-control of the old revolutionary.

Trotsky knew he had very little time left, and he did not want to waste it. He was working on a biography of Stalin, but the investigation into the Siqueiros attack itself diverted much of his attention during June and July. Meanwhile, since the ending of the Spanish Civil War in early 1939 a steady stream of GPU agents had been arriving in Mexico to join the killers (such as the American George Mink) already in position. Among the newcomers were the Argentinian V. Codovilla and the Italians Vittorio Vidali (alias Carlos Contreras) and Tina Modotti (or Maria Ruiz). David Serrano, one of the Siqueiros gang's lawyers and a member of the Political Bureau of the Mexican Communist Party, had himself served the GPU in Spain.

Left: Colonel Sanchez Salazar.
Below: Natalya shows police a slight wound sustained in the Siqueiros raid.
Bottom: Rivera and Siqueiros — would-be disciple and would-be assassin — reunited at a book launch and at Frida Kahlo's funeral in Mexico City, 1954.
Opposite page: Agents of the GPU.
Clockwise: Tina Modotti, silent movie star and photographer; George Mink; David Serrano's identity card; and Vittorio Vidali.

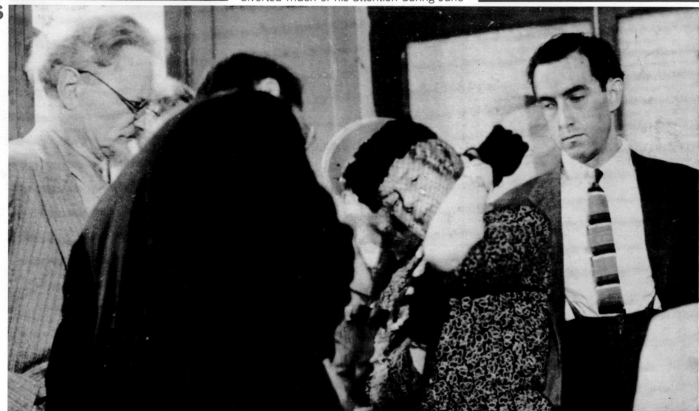

Trotsky in his study examining proofs of his unfinished biography of Stalin. Trotsky himself attached little weight to this work, which had been commissioned by a commercial publisher, but the Soviet dictator wanted it stopped.
Inset: Harold Robins, one of the guards supplied by the American SWP.

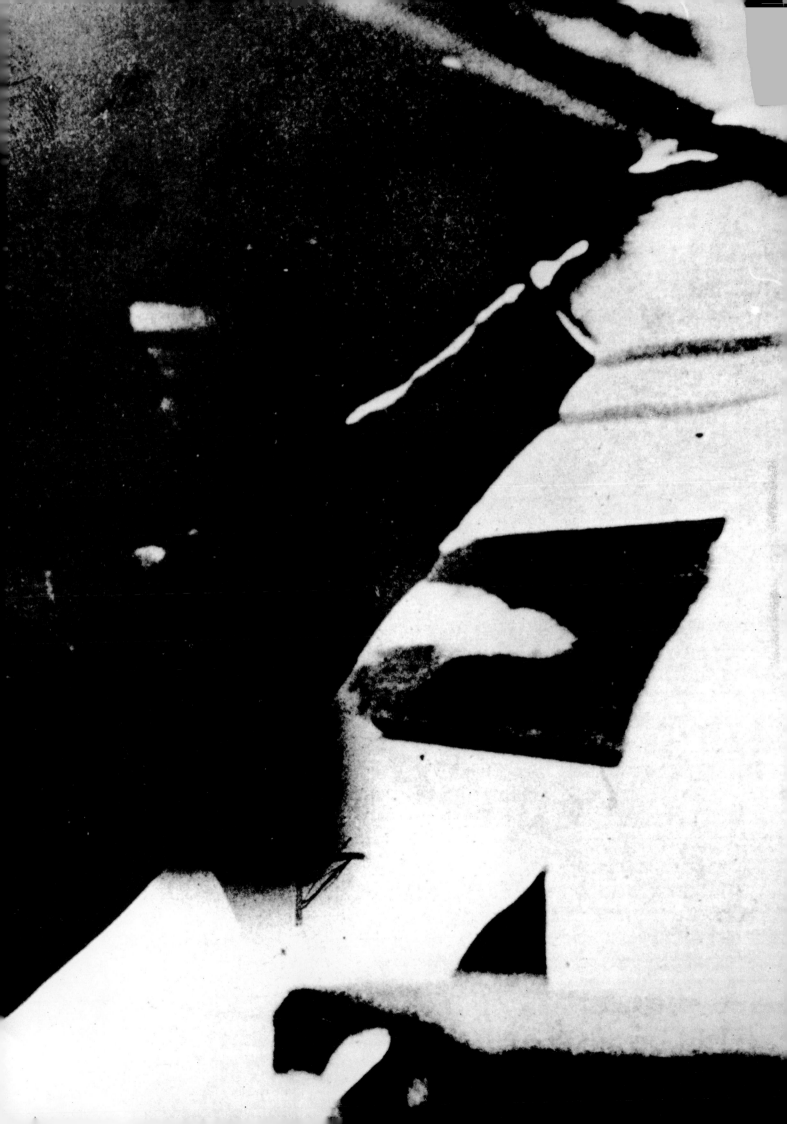

No one was allowed to feed Trotsky's rabbits except the Old Man himself. He always wore a battered pair of gloves for this purpose.

On Tuesday 20 August he got up at 7 a.m., as usual, and made his habitual joke to Natalya: 'You see, they did not kill us last night.' Feeling fit and energetic, he dressed quickly and went straight out to the rabbit hutch to tend his pets. He spent most of the morning dealing with correspondence, and then working on an article about the war. How could revolutionaries respond to the desire of US workers to fight Hitler without tying them to their own bourgeoisie?

'Our policy ... is a continuation of the policy elaborated during the last imperialist war, primarily under Lenin's leadership. But ... a continuation signifies a development, a deepening and a sharpening ... Prior to the February revolution and even afterwards the revolutionary elements felt themselves to be not contenders for power but the extreme left opposition.' Therefore they confined themselves to propaganda against the imperialist war. When it came to mobilizing the mass of the people for the seizure of state power, however, the Bolsheviks advanced a positive revolutionary slogan, 'All power to the Soviets!' The world political crisis was even sharper in 1940 than in Lenin's day. 'It is not merely a question of a position on capitalist militarism and of renouncing the defence of the bourgeois state but of directly preparing for the conquest of power and the defence of the proletarian fatherland ... '

At 1 o'clock Trotsky's lawyer came to see him, and he had to put aside his unfinished thoughts on the war. During the afternoon he worked on another, polemical article. He walked on the patio; Natalya saw him standing bare-headed in the scorching sun, and fetched his white cap. Around 5 p.m. he was back feeding his rabbits as Frank Jacson walked up to him. Jacson was the boyfriend of an American Trotskyist, Sylvia Ageloff, and a recent friend of the Rosmers. He was behaving oddly, and complained of feeling unwell. He carried a raincoat on one arm: it concealed an ice-pick. He was holding the manuscript of a small article on the Soviet Union in the other hand; he wanted Trotsky to read it over.

'Lev Davidovich was reluctant to leave the rabbits and was not at all interested in the article,' Natalya remembered. 'But controlling himself he said, "Well, what do you say, shall we go over your article?" Unhurriedly, he fastened the hutches and took off his working gloves ... He brushed his blue jacket and slowly, silently walked with myself and "Jacson" towards the house. I accompanied them to the door of L.D.'s study; the door closed and I went into the adjoining room.'

Opposite page: Trotsky reading in his garden in the Avenida Viena. Above: Feeding his rabbits.

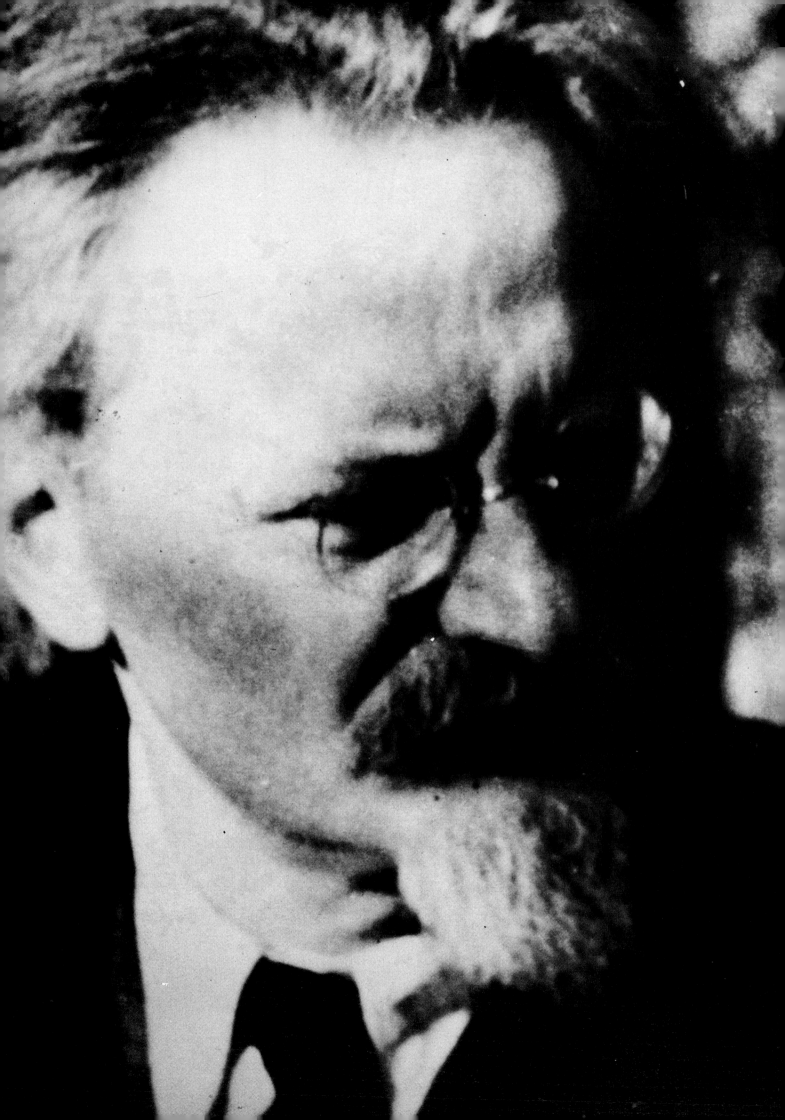

L.D. and Natalya, comrades and companions since 1902.

ASSASSINATION

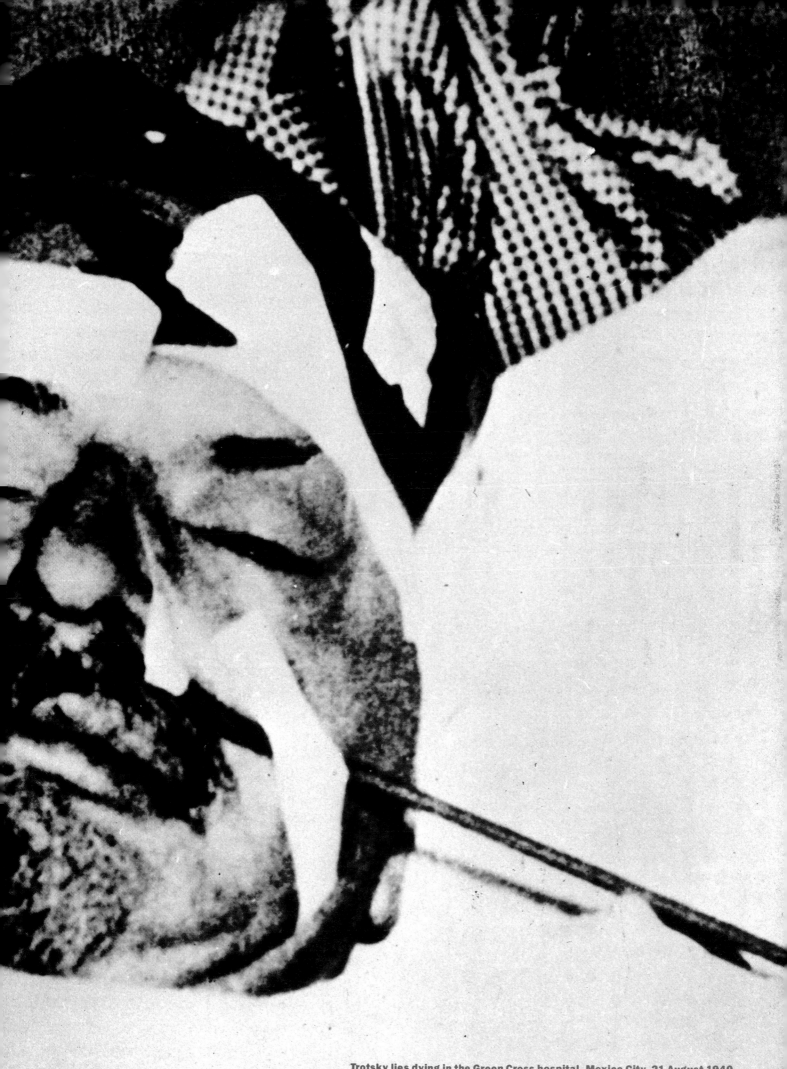

Trotsky lies dying in the Green Cross hospital, Mexico City, 21 August 1940.

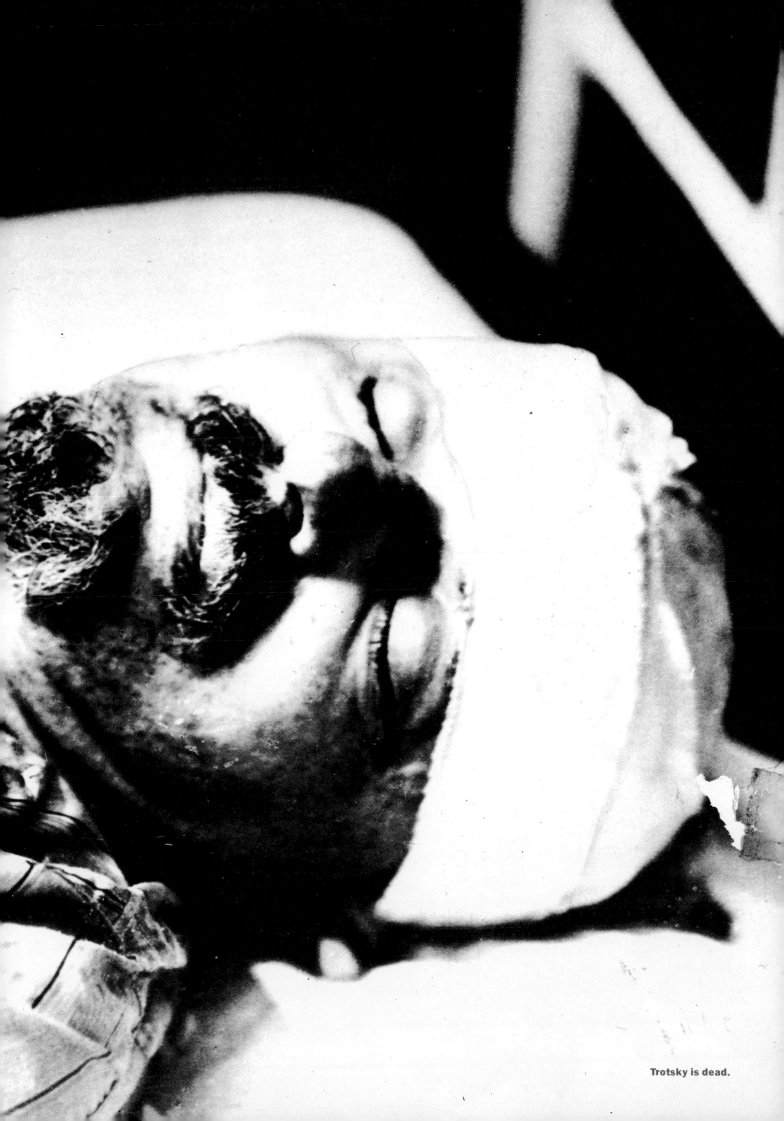

Trotsky is dead.

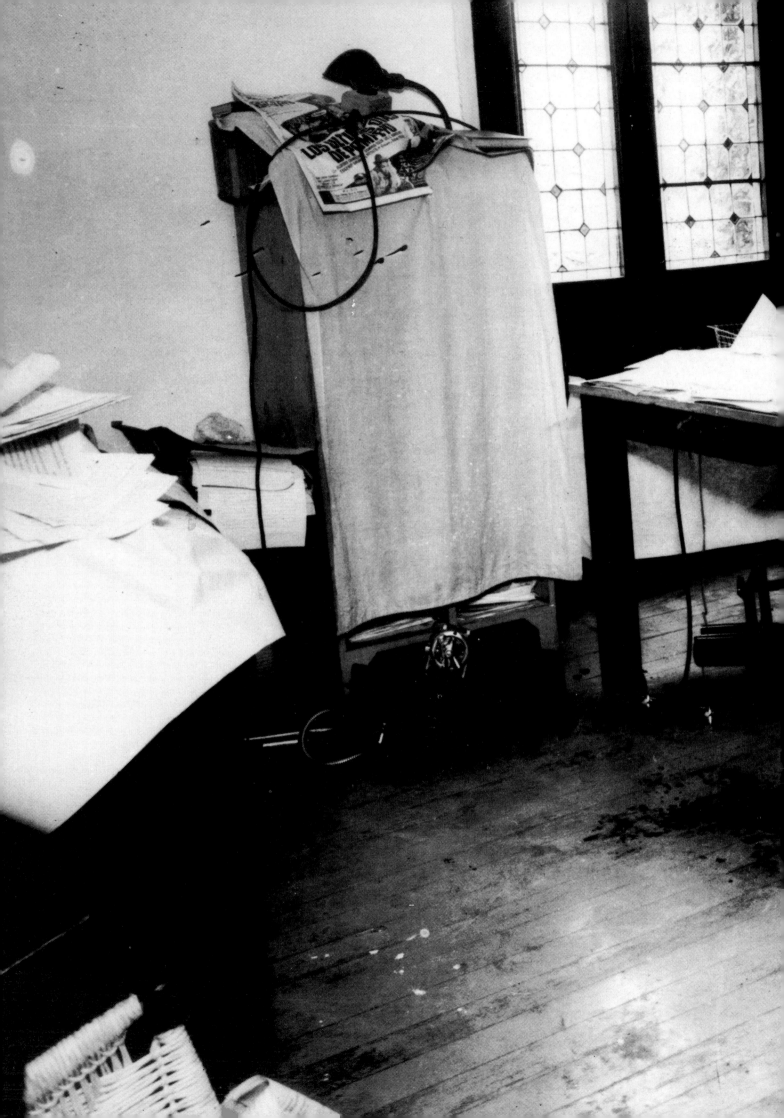

Trotsky's office as it was found after the mortal struggle with Ramón Mercader.

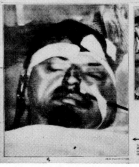

TROTSKY IS DEAD

† Trotsky Death Weapon

← Dying, He Blamed Stalin

Above: A New York newspaper reports Trotsky's assassination.
Left: Police display the murder weapon.

After he had entered his study with Jacson, Trotsky sat down at his desk and began to read the assassin's typescript. Jacson put down his raincoat, took out the ice-axe and brought it down on the old man's head with all his strength. Trotsky uttered a terrible cry and threw himself at his assailant. Jacson was so unnerved that he failed to use the revolver or dagger which he had brought. Trotsky bit his hand and wrenched away the axe, then he staggered back. Natalya, rushing into the room, found him swaying against the doorway. His blue eyes, without the glasses, shone at her through the blood that covered his face. 'I put my arms around him ... Calmly, without anger, bitterness or sorrow he said, "Jacson." He said it as if he wished to say: "Now it has happened." We took a few steps, and slowly, aided by me, he slumped down on a mat on the floor.'

The guards were beating the assassin with revolver butts; Trotsky could hear him moaning. 'Tell the boys not to kill him,' he said. 'No, no, he must not be killed — he must be made to talk.' He was struggling to articulate his words; soon his left arm and leg were paralysed. He was rushed to hospital, where doctors examined his wound. Lying on the narrow bed, he called in English to Joseph Hansen, his secretary: 'Joe, you ... have ... notebook?' And then: 'I am close to death from the blow of a political assassin ... struck me down in my room. I struggled with him ... we ... entered ... talk about French statistics ... he struck me ... please say to our friends ... I am sure ... of victory ... of Fourth International ... go forward.'

Natalya undressed him for the operating theatre, and bent over to press her lips against his. 'He returned the kiss. Again. And again he responded. And once again. This was our final farewell.' At about 7.30 p.m. he fell into a coma. He died at 7.25 in the evening of the following day.

Workers! This Is Not Our War!
It Is a War for Boss-Profits!
Join Hands in Independent
Labor Action Against the War!

LABOR ACTION

In This Issue —
LIFE OF TROTSKY
Pages 2 and 4

AUGUST 26, 1940   ORGAN OF THE WORKERS PARTY, SECTION OF THE FOURTH INTERNATIONAL   THREE CENTS

STALIN HAS MURDERED OUR COMRADE TROTSKY

Leon Trotsky has fallen. Our comrade, the great leader of the world revolution is dead. He was murdered at the dictate of Joseph Stalin.

Jacques Dreschd who wielded the axe that struck Trotsky is beyond any doubt a GPU agent. The last possible doubt was removed by the murderer's statement to the police that he had acted as he did because Trotsky had wanted him to commit acts of sabotage in Russia. So vile a lie could be mouthed only by the GPU.

Assigned the task of murdering Trotsky in the event that other attempts failed, Dreschd wormed his way into the household, pretending to be a "friend." The GPU gave him time, time to engratiate himself, time to pretend that he had been "won over" to Trotsky's views.

The Stalinists, trying to cover the trail that can lead only to themselves, will claim that Jacques Dreschd or Monord or Jackson was a "follower" of Trotsky, that he acted in disillusionment. So too they dared accuse Trotsky of himself organizing the May murder attempt. But Jacques Dreschd was not a follower of Trotsky. Jacques Dreschd was a follower, and an employee, of Stalin who has levelled the muzzle of his murder machine at the man whose very life was a challenge to the Kremlin tyrant.

One by one, that murder machine has struck down those closest to Trotsky, trying more desperately each time to strike at Trotsky himself.

Farewell, Leon Trotsky---

Our leader, teacher and comrade, Leon Trotsky is dead. Thus an historical epoch is ended. Lenin's co-worker and co-thinker, the leader of the October insurrection and the organizer of the once glorious Red Army is the last of the Old Bolsheviks.

Leon Trotsky is the victim of Cain Stalin, the gravedigger of the Russian Revolution, the assassin of brave revolutionists. For almost twelve years the Kremlin oligarch has sought to take the life of Trotsky, but each time he failed. The unspeakable GPU acting through its hireling, Von Den Dreschd finally succeeded. Gaining the confidence of our warm-hearted and genial Leon Trotsky, pretending to be a disciple of our great comrade, this scoundrel in the pay of the GPU struck down the lion of October in a brutal attack. But Joseph Stalin is the real assassin—as real as if his own hand had struck the treacherous blow.

Stalin mortally feared the man whom he had driven into exile, whose comrades he murdered, whose family he destroyed. Stalin mortally feared that the deep dissatisfaction in the Soviet Union would grow to revolutionary proportions and turn to Leon Trotsky for guidance and leadership in the overthrow of his regime of terror. Stalin mortally feared that the world working-class, unfettered by the treacherous teachings of the usurpers would turn to Trotsky and the Fourth International for leadership in the struggle against reaction and for world socialism.

Stalin's hands drip with the blood of a host of fighters for proletarian emancipation. But if he thought to wipe out the revolution, he has struck in vain! If Trotsky is no more, he has left an imperishable heritage. In the period of the degeneration of the Russian Revolution, in the triumph of reactionary Stalinism, his voice and his pen remained alive to explain and to teach a new generation of young revolutionaries to fight against the decaying order of capitalism and for the new socialist society of universal freedom for the masses of our planet.

To our brave, sorrowing comrade Natalia Ivanovna, lifelong companion of Lev Davidovitch, we extend our most heartfelt sympathy in this dreadful hour. You have been the comrade in arms of our L D for many decades and you have been our beloved comrade for many years. Your great devotion to your comrade and companion under the most perilous and trying conditions of the Russian revolutionary movement, in the gigantic events of the October insurrection and through the period of Stalinist degeneration and reaction, is a glorious lesson in revolutionary devotion and comradely sacrifice. Dear Natalia Ivan-

ovna, you are not alone! Thousands stand with you in this dark and bitter hour, sworn to carry on

Leon Trotsky, the greatest disciple of Marx, Engels and Lenin, is no more. But he lives in his heroic deeds, in his great teachings! The Kremlin Borgias has finally succeeded in his villainous deed. But let him not think that thereby he has broken the living spirit of Trotsky. There are thousands now, there will be millions tomorrow who will avenge his death. They will not only avenge the murder of our dear Leon, Trotsky. They will avenge the murder of the hundreds and thousands whom Stalin has destroyed in his counter-revolutionary ravages. They will march onward in the spirit of revolutionary Marxism, in the spirit of Lenin and Trotsky.

A new generation of revolutionaries is emerging. They will grow up in the spirit of Bolshevik courage and devotion to carry on until the victory of socialism. Under the banner of the Fourth International, founded by Leon Trotsky, the new movement will triumph. By his teachings, by his devotion and by his peerless courage in the face of the greatest dangers, the Fourth International will be nourished. Rising upon the edifice of the epoch of Lenin and Trotsky, it will sweep away the rubbish of the old order and give birth to the new movement of Socialist emancipation.

Farewell Leon Trotsky!

Hail the Fourth International!

Hail the liberating world revolution!

NATIONAL COMMITTEE, WORKERS PARTY
NATIONAL COUNCIL, YOUNG PEOPLES
SOCIALIST LEAGUE (4th International)

Left: A recent picture of Leon Trotsky taken in Mexico.

Below: Trotsky with several of his collaborators during the Russian Revolution.

AS THE LEADER OF THE RED ARMY

There was Blumkin, loyal soldier of the Russian revolution. Stalin murdered him in 1929.

There was Erwin Wolff, secretary to Trotsky, who was kidnapped and brought to Russia in 1936 by the GPU. Stalin murdered him.

There was Ignace Reiss who was found dead in Switzerland in 1937 after he had severed his connections with the reactionary GPU. Stalin murdered him.

There was Rudolph Klement, secretary to Trotsky, whose mutilated body was found in the Seine River in 1938. Stalin murdered him.

There was Sheldon Harte, bodyguard to Trotsky, who was spirited away from Trotsky's Coyoacan home when the GPU's May attack failed. Stalin murdered him.

There were the sons and daughters and countless friends of Leon Trotsky. Each of them, directly or indirectly, fell prey to Kremlin gangsterism. Only two years ago, Leon Sedov, Trotsky's son and close collaborator, suddenly died in Paris under mysterious circumstances. Stalin murdered Sedov. Stalin murdered them all.

Trotsky alive was an indomitable threat to the rotten regime of revolutionary betrayal that Stalin has foisted with knout and bullet upon the Russian masses. Each in his turn, the leaders of the glorious revolution of 1917, that liberated one-sixth of the earth until Stalin again enslaved it, have met death at the decree of Stalin. Only Trotsky, organizer of the Red Army, co-worker of Lenin, remained alive—a living challenge, epitomizing the spirit of socialism and of revolution. And now he is dead——murdered.

For twelve years, ever since he was driven by Stalin from the land whose rebellious forces he led to victory in 1917, Trotsky was the target of the GPU murder machine. They hounded him from country to country, striking at his friends and collaborators. And, finally, in Mexico, they laid fine plans for the dirty business of his assassination. George Mink, a notorious GPU agent, was in Mexico for the express purpose of organizing the murder. Last May they staged an armed assault on Trotsky's home which failed in its aim only by the merest accident.

But they had reckoned with that possibility.

(Continued on page 2)

NATALIA TROTSKY
MEXICO D F

OUR HEARTS ARE TORN WITH GRIEF OVER THE LOSS WHICH IS IRREPARABLY YOURS AND IRREPARABLY THAT OF INTERNATIONAL PROLETARIAN MOVEMENT. THE CAPTAIN OF THE WORLD ARMY OF REVOLUTION HAS FALLEN AT THE HANDS OF THE COWARDLY ASSASSIN IN THE KREMLIN. OUR FLAG IS DIPPED AT THE OPEN GRAVE OF THE IMMORTAL LEON TROTSKY. OUR DEEPEST SYMPATHY AND LOVE IS WITH YOU IN YOUR HOUR OF SORROW. LONG LIVE THE FOURTH INTERNATIONAL. LONG LIVE THE LIBERATING TRIUMPH OF THE WORKING CLASS.

WORKERS PARTY
SHACHTMAN, SECRETARY

Above: 'Labor Action', newspaper of Shachtman's breakaway group, the Workers Party, reports the assassination of Trotsky. The bourgeois press generally preferred to endorse the story — planted by the GPU — that the murder had been the work of a disillusioned follower. The Trotskyists correctly assigned the blame to Stalin and his agents. They knew some details of the plot, including several of the assassin's aliases, but his true identity was not conclusively established until 1950. Opposite page: The murderer, Ramón Mercader — alias Jacques Mornard, alias Frank Jacson, and several others — after the beating administered to him by Trotsky's bodyguards. Colonel Sanchez Salazar later recalled: 'He always gave me the impression of being an actor, a consummate actor ... He was often sarcastic. But when he was treated with firmness he became just as humble and submissive, passing from one attitude to the other with perfect control over himself. When he was questioned he became prudent and slippery.'

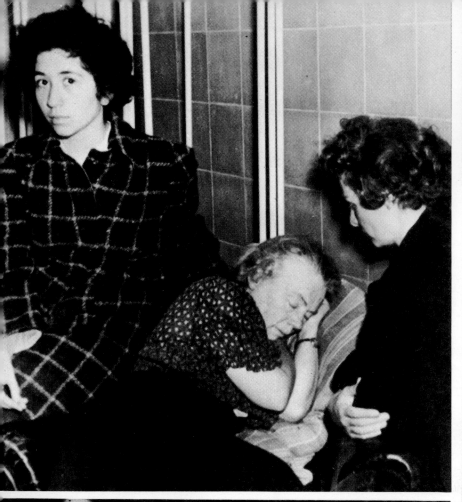

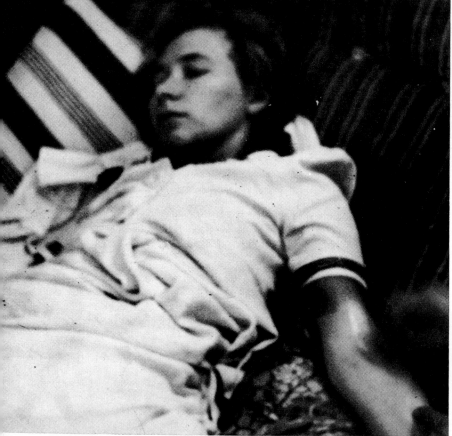

At the Avenida Viena Trotsky's guards beat out of Jacson the words: 'They have got something on me, they have imprisoned my mother ... Sylvia has nothing to do with this ...', but then he denied any connection with the GPU. He had in fact come with a ready-prepared 'confession' running to three typed pages. He claimed his real name was Jac-ques Mornard, a Belgian, and that he had become a Trotskyist in France. Trotsky, who was in the pay of an unspecified foreign power, had asked him to assassinate Stalin. Trotsky also demanded, according to Jacson, that he break with Sylvia because she sympathized with Burnham and Shachtman.

The Belgian chargé d'affaires in Mexico had no trouble showing that he was not Mornard, nor even Belgian. But it was not until 1950 that the criminologist Dr Alfonso Quiroz Cuarón proved who 'Jacson' really was.

He was born Jaime Ramón Mercader del Rio on 17 February 1914 in Barcelona. His mother Caridad left her husband in 1925 and took her children to France, where she associated with leading members of the Communist Party. Ramón was sent to Lyon to learn the hotel business. In 1932 he

enlisted in the Spanish army. In 1935 he was arrested as a member of a Communist cell. When the Civil War broke out, he became a political commissar on the Aragon front.

Caridad was sent by the Spanish republican government to Mexico as head of a delegation of Communist Party members. There she met Alfaro Siqueiros. A year later, when Siqueiros arrived in Spain as a volunteer, Caridad introduced him to her

son. Meanwhile she had become the lover of Leonid Eitingon, who headed Stalin's Division of Special Tasks in Spain. Calling himself General Kotov, Eitingon had ordered the murder of Erwin Wolf and Andrés Nin. Ramón was trained in guerrilla warfare before being taken to Moscow. In 1938 he travelled to Paris.

Above and lower left: Sylvia Ageloff in a state of shock after learning that her lover had murdered Trotsky.
Top left: Natalya waits at the hospital with two American comrades, Myra Ward (left) and Evelyn Reed, to hear if Trotsky will live.

317

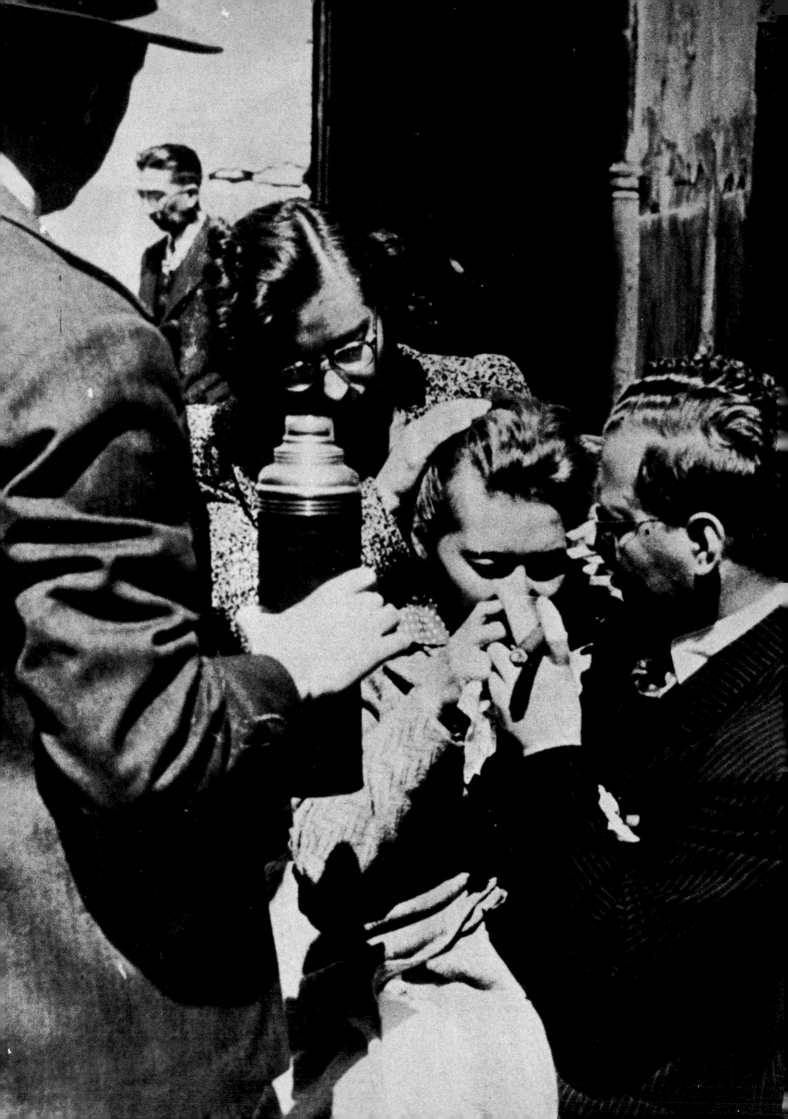

Above: Mercader under surveillance in jail shortly after the assassination.
Below: Under intense police questioning, the murderer refuses to be drawn beyond the bounds of his faked 'confession'. 'His brain worked with great agility,' Colonel Salazar later recalled. 'It was evident that he had prepared his defence very carefully. Nevertheless I made him contradict himself several times, without counting the numerous "I don't know's" and "I can't remember's" — the easy recourse of all delinquents when they are in a tight corner.'
Opposite page: Sylvia being comforted by her brother, who had hastened from New York when he heard news of the assassination and Sylvia's involvement in it.

Below: A photo taken in Paris in summer 1938, showing (left to right) Maria Craipeau (a French Trotskyist), Jacson-Mornard-Mercader and Sylvia Ageloff.
Bottom: Again in the summer of 1938, Maria Craipeau and Sylvia Ageloff (on the right) pose for the camera outside the American Express offices in Paris.
Right: Sylvia's brother tries to comfort her in the Green Cross hospital.
Below right: The confrontation in hospital between Ageloff and Mercader, arranged by Colonel Salazar. Mercader tried desperately to flee the room, and would not answer questions. 'He was crushed. He dared not look at his lover, and was obviously thinking only of how to put an end to this interview,' Salazar recalled. But he made a serious mistake by showing that he understood Spanish perfectly — yet he claimed to be a Belgian who knew little of the language, and up to that point had always been very careful not to use it.

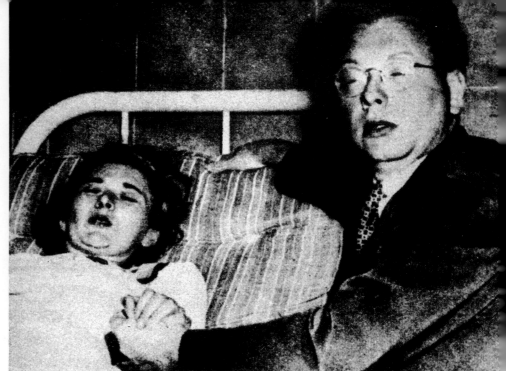

320

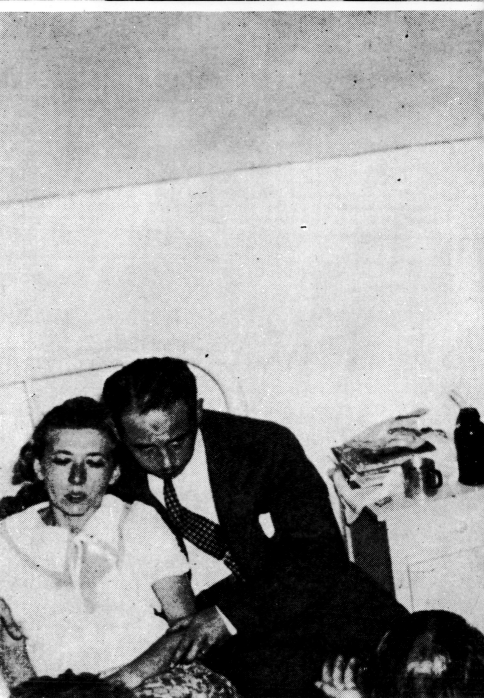

Sylvia Ageloff was one of three sisters, all Trotskyists from New York. She took a trip to Paris in summer 1938 with a new friend, Ruby Weil, who introduced her to a handsome young man, 'Jacques Mornard'. The inexperienced Sylvia was easily seduced.

'Mornard' disappeared for a fortnight in July, saying his mother had been hurt in a car accident. Sylvia went looking for him in Belgium, but he was not at the address he had given her. At this time the headless body of Rudolf Klement was found in the Seine; but Sylvia suspected nothing.

She returned to New York in February 1939. Mercader joined her in September. He now called himself Jacson and carried a false Canadian passport; he told her this was because he was evading military conscription in Belgium. In October he left for Mexico, saying he had work as a sales agent, or sometimes as a manager, for an import-export firm. She followed in February 1940. In Mexico City the couple naturally found

themselves in the company of the Rosmers. The charming Jacson took them out to dinner and drove them into the country on sightseeing trips. He also frequently gave Sylvia lifts to the Avenida Viena, where she acted as a secretary. Gradually the guards came to know him; he met Trotsky one day in the courtyard, and Natalya asked 'Sylvia's husband' (as Trotsky would refer to him) to join the family and the Rosmers at the breakfast table. On another occasion he was invited with Sylvia to tea.

He had never shown much interest in politics, except, as it were, to please Sylvia. But as the controversy with Burnham and Shachtman raged, he would occasionally venture the opinion that the Old Man was right. He was careful not to appear too eager, though he hinted to Trotsky's secretaries that he and Sylvia were having heated political arguments about the nature of the Soviet Union. As the day of the assassination neared, his behaviour became increasingly erratic. Several people, including Trotsky himself, were uneasy about him, but their

suspicions did not harden into certainty.

After his arrest Mercader maintained a stubborn silence. In an attempt to make him talk, the Mexican police arranged a confrontation with Sylvia. He was led into a hospital room where she lay sobbing. He struggled to escape while she screamed, 'Take that murderer away! Kill him! Kill him! He is a hypocrite and an assassin. I want to see him killed the way Trotsky died!' Then she turned to Mercader: 'Don't lie, traitor! Tell the truth even if you pay with your life!' And she tried to spit in his face. He seemed to be in despair, but would still say nothing, 'even if you cut my skin off inch by inch'.

For twenty years he maintained his silence in a Mexican jail. In the meantime his mother was awarded the Order of Lenin by Stalin himself, and she took away with her also the Order of Hero of the Soviet Union for her son. On his release in 1960 he went to Moscow via Havana and Prague. It is said that he died of bone cancer in Cuba in 1978.

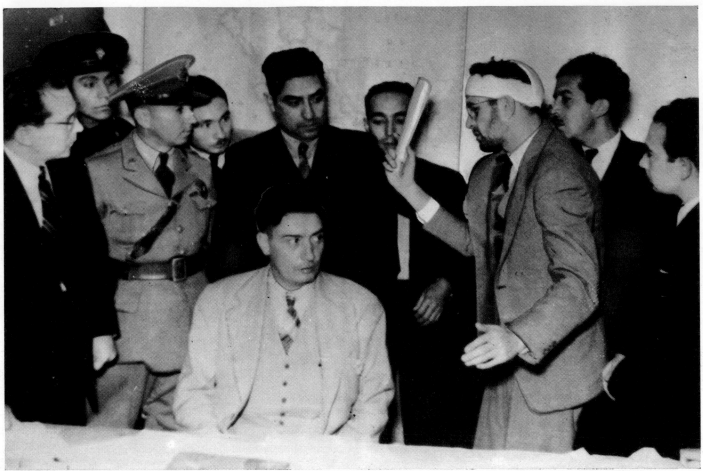

Above: On 30 August Mercader was taken under police escort to Trotsky's house to reconstruct the crime. He trembled, hunched his shoulders, hung his head and dragged his feet, 'cleverly exaggerating the weakness of his condition,' so that police officers had to half carry him. The examining magistrate broke the seals which had been placed on the door of Trotsky's study on the day of the assassination, and Mercader was led in.
He was made to re-enact the assault with a policeman taking the victim's place.
Below: Caridad Mercader with her son Ramón, dressed in the uniform of an officer in the Spanish republican army. Caridad was an agent of the GPU in Spain.
Opposite page: The proof, assembled in 1950, that the fingerprints of Ramón Mercader, taken in Spain in 1935 when he was arrested as a member of an illegal Communist cell, match those of 'Jacson-Mornard', taken in Mexico in 1940.

CUADRO QUE DEMUESTRA LA IDENTIDAD DE

RAMON MERCADER DEL RIO CON "JAQUES MORNARD"

DIRECCION GENERAL DE SEGURIDAD

ESPAÑA 1935

MEXICO 1940

INDICE DERECHO

INDICE DERECHO

27 26 25 24 23 22 21 20 19

27 26 25 24 23 22 21 20 19

REFERENCIAS

1 DELTA	10 CORTADA	19 ISLOTE
2 CORTADA	11 BIFURCADA	20 BIFURCADA
3 ISLOTE	12 HORQUILLA	21 CORTADA
4 FRAGMENTO	13 HORQUILLA	22 CORTADA
5 HORQUILLA	14 RAMA	23 CORTADA
6 CORTADA	15 CORTADA	24 CORTADA
7 CORTADA	16 CORTADA	25 FRAGMENTO
8 AISLADA	17 BIFURCACION	26 RAMA
9 CORTADA	18 CORTADA	27 CORTADA

1935 EN ESPAÑA

RAMON MERCADER

FOTOGRAFIA TOMADA DEL

PASAPORTE CON EL QUE

1940 EN MEXICO

"JAQUES MORNARD"

Crowds pack the street for Trotsky's funeral, 22 August 1940.
Opposite page: Natalya supported by the bodyguards
Harold Robins and Joseph Hansen, arriving for the funeral.
Overleaf: The procession passes through Mexico City.

Trotsky's coffin, draped in the flag of the Fourth International, is carried to the hearse; the procession passes slowly through Mexico

City; and is borne into the Pantheon, where the funeral service is to be held. Above: Joe Hansen protects Natalya from photographers.

On 22 August a funeral service was held for Trotsky in accordance with Mexican customs. A cortège followed the coffin slowly through the streets. An enormous crowd followed from the funeral parlour to the Pantheon, a distance of some eight miles. The procession passed through not only the city centre but also some of the most densely populated working-class districts in Mexico. The streets were packed on both sides with the poverty-stricken inhabitants of a city which Trotsky had come to love during the last years of his life. As the coffin approached, covered with its red flag, they took off their hats and stood silently in tribute until it had passed.

At the Pantheon three of Trotsky's comrades spoke over the bier: the American Albert Goldman, who had defended Trotsky at the hearings of the Dewey Commission; Garcia Trevino, a former leader of the Mexican trade union confederation, who made a passionate call for the labour movement to be purged of the poison of the GPU; and Grandizo Munis, a leader of the Spanish section of the Fourth International who had been incarcerated by the GPU during the Civil War.

'From August 22 to August 27 Trotsky's body was kept at the funeral parlour pending an answer from the US government to a request to take his remains to New York for a funeral service,' Joe Hansen recorded. 'A guard of honour, composed of Mexican workers and members of Trotsky's household, stood at attention twenty-four hours a day beside the casket. There was a

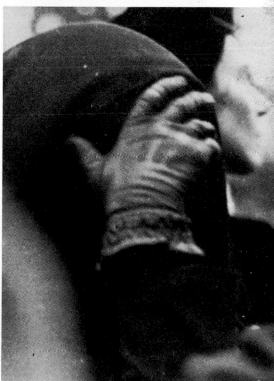

constant flow of those who wished to pay their last respects to Trotsky. By August 27 an estimated 300,000 people had passed his casket. They were composed almost entirely of the poorest people, burdened with toil, many of them ragged, barefoot. They filed in silently, heads bowed.'

Meanwhile the streets of Mexico City echoed to the strains of the anonymously composed 'Grand Corrido de Leon Trotsky': 'Murio Trotsky asesinado / de la noche a la manana / porque habian premeditado / venganza tarde o temprano ... Fué un dia martes por la tarde / este tragedia fatal / que ha conmovido al pais / y a todo la Capital.'

On 26 August the US State Department categorically refused to allow Trotsky on the soil of the United States — alive or dead. The following day his remains were cremated in accordance with his own wishes, for he was fond of saying, 'All that is fit to live is fit to perish.' The urn containing his ashes rests in the garden of the house on the Avenida Viena, Coyoacán.

Above left: Trotsky lies in state, guarded by militants of the International Communist League (Bolshevik-Leninist), Mexican Section of the Fourth International.
Above: Natalya beside the coffin (top);
Trotsky's head bearing signs of the wound which killed him (middle);
Natalya overcome with grief (bottom).
She lived on in the Avenida Viena for twenty years, and died in Paris in 1962.

The cremation. 'Let the fire consume everything that decays.'

TESTAMENT

For forty-three years of my conscious life I have remained a revolutionist; for forty-two of them I have fought under the banner of Marxism. If I had to begin all over again I would of course try to avoid this or that mistake, but the main course of my life would remain unchanged. I shall die a proletarian revolutionist, a Marxist, a dialectical materialist, and consequently an irreconcilable atheist. My faith in the communist future of mankind is not less ardent, indeed it is firmer today, than it was in the days of my youth.

Natasha has just come up to the window from the courtyard and opened it wider so that the air may enter more freely into my room. I can see the bright green strip of grass beneath the wall, and the clear blue sky above the wall, and sunlight everywhere. Life is beautiful. Let the future generations cleanse it of all evil, oppression and violence and enjoy it to the full.

L. Trotsky
Coyoacán
27 February 1940